PARADE OF HORSES

'The talk is all about horses; our
horses, other people's horses, what
might happen the day after tomorrow
if horses from other stables bump our
mare as they approach the first fence
or cross her in the act of jumping.
We wonder if we have chosen the
right races, if our luck will hold, if
there will be rain enough to soften the
ground for the big mare yet not so
much that the little hurdler and the
Irish grey will be discouraged. We
are like farmers in that we want too
many kinds of weather
simultaneously.'

This was Vian Smith's world – the
world of horses. In this book he tries
to repay the debt men owe to their
generosity and servitude through the
years.

3 cde

Also by Vian Smith

MARTIN RIDES THE MOOR
COME DOWN THE MOUNTAIN

and published by Carousel Books

Vian Smith

PARADE OF HORSES

Drawings by Michael Charlton
and photographs

CAROUSEL EDITOR: ANNE WOOD

CAROUSEL BOOKS
A DIVISION OF TRANSWORLD PUBLISHERS LTD

PARADE OF HORSES

A CAROUSEL BOOK 0 552 54022 6

Originally published in Great Britain
by Longman Group Limited

PRINTING HISTORY
Longman edition published 1970
Carousel edition published 1972
Carousel edition reprinted 1974

Carousel Books are published by Transworld Publishers Ltd.,
Cavendish House, 57–59 Uxbridge Road,
Ealing, London, W.5

Made and printed in Great Britain by
Cox & Wyman Ltd., London, Reading and Fakenham

CONTENTS

ILLUSTRATIONS

Vian Smith and Silver Fiddle, the steeplechaser (*Photo, H. R. Rivers*)

The rosinbacks (*Radio Times Hulton Picture Library*)

The Exmoor (*IPC Magazines*)

The pair (*Radio Times Hulton Picture Library*)

The author and Juliet, the Dartmoor pony (*Photo, H. R. Rivers*)

The barge horse (*Radio Times Hulton Picture Library*)

The cutting horse (*Photo, Ed Smyth*)

'The Horse of Selene' from the Parthenon frieze (*British Museum*)

The English thoroughbred (*Sport and General Press Agency*)

Exercising on the sands (*Photos, H. R. Rivers, and IPC Magazines*)

For Gaenor and Ricky
In memory of holidays in Devon

I

HORSES IN THE GREEN VALLEY

IT'S still night in the sky, but in the boxes there's a
harvest colour; richer at six than it will be at seven when
the pressure of darkness begins to lift and the chimneys
of the house begin to show.

The horses come to their half doors and smell the
morning. For months they've been trotted and cantered,
walked up steep hills, schooled over hurdles and fences,
galloped on tidal sands when the sounds of the sea have
withdrawn. For as long they've been fed the best corn,
the best hay; daily rations of nuts and honey, of carrots

and beans, weekly rations of boiled linseed and cod liver oil and malt. Now they're almost ready and know it and react in their various manners: the Irish grey excited, the four-year-old hurdler petulant, the big brown mare bold and arrogant and demanding.

The last head to show is the bay gelding with the long black legs, veteran of many steeplechases during which he never fell and scarcely faltered. He was bought years ago to give my young sons confidence over fences. Now he schoolmasters young horses over hurdles and ditches. He stares at the morning as though he owns it. My daughters call him 'King'.

We straighten their night-rugs and fork out muck dropped during the night. This isn't only a chore. It's an opportunity to assess their well-being. Loose muck suggests chill or extreme anxiety, or oats not fully mature. Inadequate muck suggests constipation and can be cured in one horse by ten minutes of grass; in another by liquid paraffin; in a third by the salts which were discovered in a stream near Epsom in 1618, establishing that village as a health resort long before it became a horse-town.

We bring the food buckets while mares in foal peer in entreaty and the Exmoor pony wags her head and nuckers and clobbers the door with her forefeet. Breakfast for horses in training is the smallest meal of the day; two pounds of lightly crushed oats, sprinkled with a little bran. For hunting ponies it is damp bran and a proprietary brand of nuts. Mares in foal have stud nuts which help to supply essential minerals. The Dartmoor pony peers through the gate, reminding us that size is no measure of importance, so could we hurry, please? My sons and daughter palm her whatever is in their pockets and the Exmoor mare turns jealous.

Stable cats ooze down from the lofts and come around, tails erect to claim attention, their bodies inclined for rubbing. They get bowls of bread and milk in winter, for it's a fallacy that cats hunt only when they are hungry. These are she-cats and because they are strong as well as fast, always about to have kittens or nursing kittens or mourning the loss of kittens, they hunt vermin with persistent ferocity; seeming to be jungle animals in miniature as they carry their prey to secret places among bales of hay or straw.

Yet they show discrimination in their hunting. They ignore the fat, white pigeons which scrounge shreds of corn, having reached a truce with them, as the yellow labrador accepts the tame partridge among the hens and the one-eyed pheasant in the orchard. Twice a year mallards bring their young from marshes near the stream, the young stretched in line astern like a show of strength in the Mediterranean. On these occasions, cats and dog are acutely embarrassed and pretend to be asleep; contriving even to ignore the strutting drake, which wants everyone to come and see.

Lights appear in the house and the windows are transformed by the promise that breakfast is not only for animals. Two taps on a pane mean two minutes; three taps mean you're late. We go in to the smell of warmth and show our cold to the flames and take our places at the long table where field-workers used to sit when this was a farmhouse. Each member of the family has a place and no other sits in it, even though the son or daughter might be absent for months or a year.

One of our sons is home from London. He will ride the big brown mare in a steeplechase the day after tomorrow. He is concerned about his weight and confines breakfast to toast and a small cup of coffee. This afternoon he will put on four sweaters and run the steep fields, then step on the scales and groan because the last pounds are the worst.

My elder daughter is home from college in Yorkshire. She holds up her plate for more, calling it 'Mother's breakfast', which seems to be vitally different from any other. The talk is all about horses; our horses, other people's horses, what might happen the day after tomorrow if horses from other stables bump our mare as they approach the first fence or cross her in the act of jumping. There is anxiety behind the small talk. We wonder if we have chosen the right races, if our luck will hold, if there will be rain enough to soften the ground for the big mare yet not so much that the little hurdler and the Irish grey will be discouraged. We are like farmers in that we want too many kinds of weather simultaneously.

Breakfast is over at a quarter to eight. The younger daughter helps her mother to clear the table and wash up, hurrying over it because the horses will be out soon and Mother will want to watch. Mother does not like racing. She 'watches' with her eyes closed, considering the safe return of horse and son to be a kind of victory. But she likes watching the stages of preparation.

In the stables the rugs are taken off and the cats move in, claiming the warmth of the rugs and curling into it. On cold mornings they will not give it up readily and have to be shaken out. The horses are brushed over; their feet cleaned; their eyes and nostrils sponged. Exercise sheets and wither pads are placed beneath the saddles. The horses pull faces as the girths tighten. My daughter is panting reproaches to the veteran because he is an actor, glaring and grimacing like the villain of old-fashioned melodrama. The four-year-old hurdler squeals. The big mare kicks. The dog moves unconcernedly behind her to share a night-rug with the senior cat.

The veteran leads them out with lordly stride, flirting

his head on a long rein while younger horses buck and sidle. They go up the hill to the exercise field, where three flights of hurdles have been erected along one straight hedge, three schooling fences beside another. They will not jump today. They will use the track marked by white hurdles and periodically rolled to keep in the rain. Twice a week my wife and I pore over this track like beachcombers, stooping for stones and replacing divots. Hundreds of hours have to be invested if you are to keep your horses safe.

We test the earth, assessing the firmness and the risks of injury to feet or tendons. There is no dew and that's a good sign. We listen to the nut trees and that's another; for the dried leaves are rustling upward in readiness for rain. We say the trees are talking about rain and tell our sons and daughter to listen. But they can hear only the breathing of the horses and the chime of bit-rings as heads go up and down in an impatient rhythm.

The horses turn away and begin to canter on tight reins; their eyes down and heads drawn in, their nostrils swollen in resentment of restraint. The faces of the riders are grim. Their bodies are crouched in concentration. They are waiting for the oak trees which mark the half-mile. As they pass the oaks they will begin to 'stretch on', quickening up the gradual incline to complete the mile.

The veteran knows what is coming and anticipates the trees, beginning to stretch five strides early to the alarm of our daughter who is afraid of being 'carted'. For a few strides the veteran is in front and alight with glee. Then younger horses come on either side and their strides are matched as they come up the incline. They go

by us in a controlled huddle and begin to slow. We wait
for them to turn and to trot back. They walk around us
while my wife plucks shreds of grass and distributes
them like congratulations.

I listen to their breathing. In the classic phrase 'they
wouldn't snuff a candle'. I pass behind, looking for cuts
or spreading shoe, for any hint of injury to legs or feet.
Our daughter says, 'Nearly pulled my flaming arms
out.' It's a jubilant boast. There's a feeling of optimism
and in that moment my wife decides to have champagne
in readiness, for you never know.

The next hour is busy. Saddle patches and girth
marks are sponged and scraped. The horses are walked
around, wearing perforated sheets until the stains are
dry. Meanwhile, soiled straw is forked out and new
forked in. Water buckets and hay-nets are refilled. The
horses are led in for brushing. The dog gets up at once,
aware of what must happen; but the cats have to be
shaken out before rugs can be replaced. Head-collars are
removed. The horses are free to drink, to pluck hay, to
peer above their half doors at the fantails on the roofs or
to hear the diabolical chuckling of the pheasant in the
orchard.

It is ten o'clock and one part of the day is ending.
Mares in foal are led to the meadow. Our sons ride hunting ponies to meet friends from neighbouring farms.
Our daughter takes her books to the tack-room and
reads as she cleans equipment which will be needed
the day after tomorrow. My wife goes back to being the
mother of a large family in a large house. I go to the
room which looks on the garden and the ancient tree and
the stone walls where birds nest in spring. This room is

small and warm. It is lined with books and littered with
papers crushed up in disgust. The papers are deepest
near the desk and I come to it slowly, for I've a book to
write and the next chapter will not come.

Non-fiction, the publishers suggested. For young
readers. All about horses, past and present. But there
have been so many horses, representing so many breeds;
so many books recounting the same facts about those
breeds. I want this book to be different but I don't know
how to do it.

None can help a writer through his problems. He can
do little to help himself; only lean back and smoke and
look around and wait. I look around the garden and
nothing happens. I look around the room and nothing
happens, except that my eye chances on a calendar. It
has illustrations. Each illustration is a month and it is
my good fortune that the illustration for this month is of
horses ploughing.

They are Shire horses. They come out of history with
ears pricked and faces serious, and far in the background
I can hear the ploughman calling and the seagulls
crying. It's many years since pairs worked regularly like
this in the fields of Britain, but this is what the nostalgic
want to remember. You are meant to believe this was
how it used to be in the days before machines.

It's not what I remember. I look at this proud pair
and what I remember is winter mud and stinging rain
and one horse drawing wooden wheels along lanes rutted
deep by storms. The horse is Pleasant. Five minutes ago
I had supposed her forgotten but now she's coming into
focus, so that I can smell her sweat and the rain in her
mane. Gradually it's the late 1920s and I am seven years

old and staying with my grandparents who had a meagre farm on the hills of Dartmoor in south-west England. I can hear the old man hollering; to the sheep and the dog, the calves and the steers, sometimes to me, but never to Pleasant. He spoke to her in a special voice and the special voice told me how important she was to him and my grandmother and to the future of the farm.

Now I know what the next chapter is going to be about. I reach for a pad of paper and write 'The Farm Horse' in block letters. Such a title makes Pleasant more than an old bay mare. It makes her representative of a type, perhaps the most important in the history of British agriculture.

2

THE FARM HORSE

HORSES began to be used for heavy work on farms in the sixteenth century when changes in agriculture, beginning with the enclosure of land, demanded deeper ploughing and the gradual substitution of horses for oxen. The Suffolk Punch became the 'great horse' of East Anglia, the Clydesdale of Scotland, the Cleveland of Yorkshire. They are proud breeds and tradition pretends they bore the burden of a developing nation on their backs.

It wasn't as simple or as spectacular as that. The best horses have always cost big money and those men of town and village and isolated farm who could not afford the best used native ponies: the Fell and Dale of Northern England, the Highland of Scotland, the mountain breeds of Wales; small animals but strong, versatile and willing, giving more than twenty years of steady service before their strength faded and their legs collapsed. They were still being used in the first half of the twentieth century, for it was not until the 1939–45 war that tractors trundled into the fields to end more than four hundred years of the horse's reign.

The period which I remember best is the late 1920s; a bleak period for the small farmer because of poverty in towns and men out of work in industrial areas. The wealthy could still have teams of Shires ploughing new earth and drawing reapers through summer wheat, but most of the farms were small, most of the farmers struggling. Their stock was poor by modern standards. They kept a few dairy cows and sold milk locally. They kept a few steers and pigs, perhaps a hundred sheep. Miscellaneous hens laid in carts and nettles, and the eggs were worth a penny each or elevenpence for a dozen. The most important animal on the farm was the horse which needed to be plough-horse one day, cart-horse the next and was harnessed to the trap on market-days.

Such a one was Pleasant, the cross-bred mare which belonged to my grandfather. She was his only horse. His dependence on her was absolute. In a strange way he trusted her never to go lame or sick or to show the weaknesses prevalent among other horses. His word for her was 'hard'. It was the greatest compliment, for countrymen in all parts of the world, the peasants of Turkey no less than the prairie farmers of North America, have always respected hardiness above all else.

Pleasant worked in mud and wind, in rain which stung her eyes until they were swollen and bruised like plums. She changed colour with sweat during the long days of summer, and when each day was done she walked without guidance to the stream. I learned then that a working horse must always drink before it eats, for a horse has a small stomach capacity in relation to its size and if it drinks after it has eaten or alternates food with drink, it will flush through the food, deriving little benefit and perhaps suffering colic.

Pleasant drank in a refined and delicate way; not gulping like some horses nor lapping noisily like a dog nor with ticking tongue like a cat. Her mouth made a smiling shape on the water so that you couldn't be sure. She might be teasing, for Pleasant knew I was waiting to walk back with her and even in her tiredness she had a sense of humour.

When Pleasant had had enough of drinking or teasing, she drew back from the stream, never stepping into it or muddying her drinking place. It was another sign of her delicacy. As I trotted beside her, taking three strides while she took one, she seemed to be very tall and wise. Now and again she darted a glance, permitting me to be alongside provided I did not attempt to guide.

She needed no guidance to the stable in a corner. It was as dark as a hovel but she gave it dignity, making it superior to the place for calves next door. Her mood changed as she went in. She no longer wanted company, for the stable meant the trough and the trough meant food and Pleasant liked privacy when she was eating.

Bran and black oats were her evening feed. There was hay in the rack, stuffed down from the loft above. But she was also partial to a mangold, thrown into the wooden trough with the earth still on it. She ate the earth as she sank her front teeth into it and such apparent crudity surprised me, for she could be fussy in other ways. I didn't know until much later that she got salt out of the earth and that all horses need a steady supply. She didn't lie down at night. She hung her head and slept where she stood, asking remarkably little in return for all she gave.

She gave from dawn to dusk and because of her reputation for toughness and willingness, other hill-farmers were glad to buy her offspring, paying perhaps three pounds for a youngster which would not be worked until it was four. This money was important to my grandfather and Pleasant had a series of foals in the years which I remember.

The gestation period for a foal is eleven months and Pleasant was mated in May so that the foal would be born the following April, when the grass was green and the weather mild. The stallion was one of those which travelled the rural places in those days, led by a groom who had bowed legs and a wizened face and who wore a yellow waistcoat. The fee was one pound, transformed into a guinea by a shilling for the groom. A guinea always seemed a most impressive sum to me, worth more than twenty-one shillings.

Pleasant was worked when she was fat and until foaling was imminent. This was not considered harsh. Moorland women worked to within an hour of confinement, partly of necessity, partly because they'd learned from other generations that a woman who worked up to the time of delivery suffered less than one made soft by pampering. It did not seem unreasonable that animals should do what humans practised and my memory is that working mares delivered easily and with few complications, provided they were given privacy in the last hours.

I remember once when Pleasant foaled. My grandfather had been watching her all day, encouraging her to keep moving yet plainly apprehensive. Several hours earlier than usual he took off the harness and opened the gate to the orchard, allowing her to pass towards her favourite corner where old trees stooped to make premature darkness. He turned away and made me turn away, not in indifference but because mares hate to be watched. Some will even hold the foal, cramping their muscles in a refusal which might be ancient instinct, remembered from ten thousand years ago when horses lived in fear of being hunted. It also explains why so many foals are born at night, when darkness makes secrecy absolute.

Pleasant foaled during the night with none to help or interrupt. In the morning the foal was there, wobbling on legs absurdly long, like the legs of a caricature. Its face was puckered in bewilderment, but Pleasant's expression was calm and warm. She darted a smiling glance, asking us to observe and admire. I made the best audience because I was the most easily impressed. It seemed a miracle to me and so it was; for every birth takes us back to the beginning, to the essential mystery which has fascinated man since he first began to wonder.

I remember another incident that summer. Pleasant was returning from market, a journey of about eight

miles. The sky was red, the moorland hills were purple.
Clouds were stretched like wings going home. Pleasant
was also going home. She strained to trot every yard,
even the longest hill, compelled by an instinct more demanding than any man could have been. My grandfather knew what was in her head. He always clucked
his tongue when he was nervous and he clucked all the
time as her hooves struck sparks and the trap rocked and
the smell of her sweat came back to the driving seat.

She reached the hill above the farm and stopped,
looking down to the roofs and the yard, to the twisted
trees of the orchard. Suddenly she neighed. I had never
heard such a sound. It seared itself into my memory, so
that I can still hear it; shrill with entreaty and authority
and worry. The foal answered and Pleasant shrieked
again, assuring it that she was coming. My grandfather
tried to hold her but she was beyond restraint.

She plunged down the hill, heedless of the mad
bounce of the wheels. The gate to the yard was open.
The trap swayed between granite posts and clattered to
the cobbles. My grandfather was old and usually slow,
inclined to grumble about the pains in his legs and back.
But he was quick this time, rejuvenated by alarm because in this mood Pleasant might kick the trap to
pieces.

The traces fell, the shafts went down. Pleasant tried to
run, resisting his attempts to get off harness and bridle,
looking up to the sounds of the foal as she shrilled
another neigh. I remember the red flare of her nostrils,
the madness in her eyes.

'Open the gate,' my grandfather shouted.

I raced to the orchard and barely made it. She

reached the gate as it began to open and blundered
through, running like a young mare, made young by a
fury which brushed me aside like nothing. The sounds
she made to the foal were soft and confiding. She drifted
her nostrils over it, making sure it was all right, not
sullied by any other smell. When she was sure, she
arranged her body carefully and widened her back legs
and let it grope, flattening her ears in reproach of
clumsiness, then sighing as the foal found what she had
to give.

I watched what happened. Her fury faded like light
from the sky and her head began to heavy down, her
lower lip drooping. Within minutes she was old. You
couldn't believe she had trotted eight miles and frightened my grandfather or had looked capable of jumping
the gate if it didn't open quickly enough.

I remember staying near the orchard, vowing that

some day it would be different. She wouldn't have to keep on giving. She would receive; the best stable and the best food, years of retirement in which she could have her foals and never be separated during the important months. I must have been seven years old and you make big vows when you are seven, sure you can do anything as soon as you are old enough.

Of course Pleasant died – found dead in that secret corner of the orchard – long before I could do more than watch and promise, but the time came when I was able to give other horses all that I'd promised to give her.

It is a way of making amends, but it isn't enough. I still feel ashamed and sad, because in thousands of years men have taken from horses more, much more, than through poverty or ignorance or neglect they have contrived to give back.

3

THE CIRCUS

IT'S a patch of waste land where the irises grow. It's all that remains of the acre where the circus used to be.

Ours was a small market town, so it did not qualify for a big circus. It made do with those which toured the green country in days when the radio was wireless and films were silent and cars were as few as birds in winter. May to September was the tenting season. The circus came for two days and four performances. You could get in for sixpence, for half price if you were young enough. You could also get in for nothing, which is what I had to do.

I remember the last to come. It came from a town twelve miles away and no one believed the advance pub-

licity, which promised a stupendous attraction. Its
wagons were drawn by brown and white skewbalds and
black and white piebalds with smaller ponies hitched to
the back of each wagon, their feet pattering to keep up
like children beside their fathers. The smallest was no
more than nine hands high, instantly recognizable as the
'Joey'; the clown's pony which would butt the ringmaster and steal his hat and represent mischief to a
young audience.

The wagons were driven by the father and his two
sons. Mother and daughters sat beside them; dark
haired and brown, not recognizable as the girls who
would become tight-rope walkers and acrobats and
bare-back riders. We walked beside the wagons to the
patch of waste land, half afraid of the circus family because they were foreign and had foreign skills, yet fascinated by what they represented. They represented
something denied to us by school walls and empty
pockets and by parental authority. They represented
freedom, by which we meant new places and staying up
late and getting away from the neighbours.

They seemed not to notice us or to care about our
fascination. They drove the wagons to a corner of the
waste land and got down swiftly. No orders were given
by the father or needed by his sons and daughters. They
knew what to do while the mother remained in the
wagon, fat and busy and sometimes singing. It was a
strange song. It seemed to come out of the long ago,
when nomad families first took their performing
animals across Europe.

The sons released the horses from the shafts and tethered them on long ropes for grazing. This evening

piebalds and skewbalds would become 'rosinbacks', the name of the stuff which trickriders used to give their feet a firmer grip. But the ponies were not tethered. They wandered with lengths of rope dangling from their necks. When one stepped on a rope it was momentarily checked and this frequent interruption reminded it that it was only on parole. The Joey had no rope. He grazed alone, his ears flattening if you came near. You could see that the impudent comedian which audiences were meant to love was in private petulant and moody.

Two terriers lay in the shade of a wagon. This evening they would play a kind of tennis, bouncing a ball across a low net and barking in excitement as they reached for the high ones. Until then they would remain tethered as sheepdogs are confined to ensure their keenness when they are released. I felt sorry for the dogs and remembered what my mother had said about circus animals living 'unnatural lives', compelled to do 'unnatural tricks' and governed by fear. Yet when I ventured close enough to see their faces, the terriers did not seem cowed or afraid. They were watching the daughter who had trained them, their eyes bright and ears awake, like collies which wait for the whistle.

The tent breathed up and the sons hammered stakes while the daughters fixed wooden tiers around the ring in readiness for a full house. I wanted to warn them. The day was Friday, pay-day for the workers of saw mill and corn mill and therefore a good day, but the town wasn't impressed by what the circus family had to offer. They were out of date. I'd heard my parents say so. Our town had a picture-house now and some families had the wireless. We no longer needed the old tricks and familiar clowning which were all a small circus could offer.

At midday the circus family gathered on the steps of a wagon and ate and drank, talking seldom, smelling of sunshine and dust and tiredness. The father sat on the top step, his hair grey and his face deeply lined; seeming no different from the tired men of our town yet made different by his skills, by his freedom from rates and neighbours and bosses, by the rootlessness which meant that although he knew everywhere, he belonged nowhere, always on the outside of the small towns. Once he might have been a juggler and acrobat, apparently fearless on the trapeze. In his middle years he might have been a clown. Now he had passed those accomplishments to his sons and was the boss which meant he was also ringmaster and horsemaster, farrier and veterinary surgeon. His veterinary treatment needed to be quick if the circus was to be kept moving.

When a horse had a poisoned foot, he covered bread with boiling water and placed the steaming pulp in a sack, drawing it over the hoof and tying it around the leg. If the injury was a bruised tendon he led the horse to a stream and stood beside it in the shallows, stroking its long sad face as the cold fanned around the leg and reduced the swelling. Every day brought its crisis and every day he had to find an answer without spending money. Today it was a wagon wheel and he had to be a wheelwright.

The sons helped him repair it while the mother and daughters scrubbed clothes and hung them on lines between the wagons. They seemed remarkably disciplined and humble, much more versatile than those of the town who condemned them vagrants and illiterates. I inched closer, making it plain that I didn't want only to get in for nothing.

They let me help with the horses. The sunshine which warmed the girls' laundry and blessed the hayfields was savage to the horses. They aimed their tails and shook their manes, but the black flies of summer do not only harass. They bite and raise great lumps, clustering in the corners of a horse's eyes and drinking the tears. Horseflies as brown as shreds of old leaf, pierce the skin and suck blood. They are disgusting things and it's a merciful hand which swipes them.

I stood near the oldest rosinback, swatting and counting and making great gestures in the air. He knew what I was doing and leaned closer, rubbing his tears against my shoulder when I had to wait a minute because my arm was dropping off. Half-way through the afternoon two others came near enough to benefit from the service, but the Joey wanted help from none. He crept to the side of a wagon and kept his tail sniping. Meanwhile other ponies formed their own community, standing nose-to-tail so that the tail of one cleaned the face of another.

You knew it was nearly time when the ponies came towards the wagons, as punctual for the first performance as cows for milking. They had decorations on their surcingles and bridles, but sunlight exposed the shoddiness and took all pretence of splendour out of the plumes which the rosinbacks wore to make them seem taller. I began to wonder how long the family could continue. They must have known the days of the small circus were almost over, yet there was no surrender in their talk. The younger daughter was asking when she could attempt in public the back-somersault which she had achieved in private. Her father said not yet, as though there was plenty of time.

He put on the hat which was the symbol of authority and which a clown would knock off for the Joey to steal. The Joey came fussily towards the tent, shaking his bells to claim attention. The mother dressed the dogs. They wore green skirts and the dog which always won leered at the girl who had trained them, eager for the game to begin. Sons came from the caravan, transformed by grotesque paint and ginger wigs, by clown clothes which had water-jets in the lapels and trick flowers in the pockets. The daughters wore tinselled skirts and had paper flowers in their hair. One of them took the dogs; the other rubbed her satin shoes in rosin like a boxer before the first round. Their mother came to her place at the flap. They waited for the customers.

I wanted to explain but they didn't look at me. They looked up the hill and waited twenty minutes. Their faces showed neither surprise nor humiliation, but I felt their contempt of those who supposed that shadows on a screen and voices in a box could be a substitute for living skills. The sons and daughters watched their father, waiting for him to decide. He waited five more minutes, then beckoned the mother to raise the flap, the younger daughter to bring the rosinbacks. He passed into the tent and cracked his whip and the rosinbacks began to go round and round, their strides matched, as monotonous as jaws chewing gum.

The sons came to the centre of the ring, calling encouragement to their sister as she ran beside the leading horse and sprang and sat and stood and raised a leg,

performing elementary tricks in preparation, her face
pale, a corner of her mouth creased in a tremor, her
brothers crying wordless sounds like warriors as she slid
from the broad back and retreated until she was standing beside her father in the centre of the ring. She
needed a roll of drums to celebrate the tightening of her
courage. I was near enough to see the sweat on her top
lip.

Her father cracked the whip and the rosinbacks went
round twice while she leaned and waited, waited too
long, running forward and faltering and coming back to
her father who was ready to call it off if she wasn't sure.
She shook her head and leaned again, beginning to run
while the leading rosinback was several strides away.
She reached it and swung and rose and straightened,
fiddling her feet backward until she was standing between loins and hip, her arms out on either side, her
body breathing with the rhythm.

Her mother made the sign of the Cross as she watched
from the flap. Her brothers looked up, their anxieties
showing through the grinning paint. Her father
watched the horses. They all trusted the horses. If one of
them faltered or changed its stride, she would fall and
break her back.

The horses were concentrating, their heads drawn in
by short side reins, their eyes down, only their ears
moving to show they were waiting for the instant of
decision. The girl decided. Her body rose and began to
turn. The arc seemed not to be high enough or brave
enough. The soft young body seemed doomed and for a
moment quicker than a blink, I imagined her sprawling,
as broken as a bird. But she made it, somehow she made

it. Her feet found the back of the second horse, her body wobbled, her arms went out; the fright in her face showed how close she was to falling. She swayed and stayed there while her brothers cheered and her mother clapped and the rosinbacks pounded a rhythm which seemed to quicken in relief.

It wasn't a new trick. It had been performed by Cossacks and Hungarians, perhaps by the Persians eight thousand years ago; but her panting made it seem new, a wonderful achievement. She circled the ring twice, holding out her arms to the empty benches, then sliding down and running to her father.

She was his favourite. I sensed that in the subtle something which passed between them; a matching of smiles as though triumph had been created out of the nothing which the town had given. The rosinbacks slowed and stopped and nodded their plumes. She palmed each a cube of sugar. She was still patting them when the dressed up dogs came dancing in with jubilation.

It was the only performance which this family gave in our town. In the morning they hitched the horses which had been rosinbacks and the town watched them go with relief, because even those with wirelesses felt guilty about the empty tent. Few remember them now, but when I come to the place where the irises grow like flowers on a grave, I wonder what happened to the father who had to be veterinary surgeon and farrier and wheelwright; to the sons who had inherited a dying tradition; to the mother who had clapped. I wonder most about the daughter, if she ever repeated that trick to the applause of a hot and crowded tent. You fall in love easily when you are ten and I think I must have fallen in love with her when I realized her fright and how close she was to falling.

Perhaps that's why I remember the horses which saved her; remember them so clearly that for me the king of circus horses is not the high school specialist or the Arab stallion or the Joey pony running off with someone's hat and everyone's laughter. It's the trustworthy rosinback, pounding round and round with head drawn in and eyes serious, waiting for the moment of decision.

4

THE EXMOOR

SHE should be called Big Ben, having a similar regard for punctuality. When you're five minutes late, she neighs and listens and gives another minute. Her second neigh is much less tolerant, her third is authoritative, her fourth a bullying sound, followed by a murmurous grumbling like an old woman asking herself what things are coming to. When your footsteps come at last, she grunts and paws her door, demanding to be first because she's the eldest and has been here the longest and such qualifications count at feed time.

She's an Exmoor pony and my sons learned to ride on her. She's strong and broad and likes to bustle and when I touch her head, I let my hand go down the determined face to the pale muzzle. Officially it's described as 'mealy'. In fact it's the colour of putty with the linseed oil still showing. History is in this muzzle, warm there and alive. Take a long look at it, for this is where it all began.

Until 1881, none could be sure where it began, but in that year Colonel N. M. Przewalski found in the highlands of Central Asia the skin and skull of a truly wild horse. It was named *Equus przewalski* in his honour and was subsequently described as being 'intermediate in character between the horse on the one hand, the kiang and onager on the other'. Twenty years later Carl Hagenbeck, of Hamburg, financed an expedition which found scattered herds in the Gobi desert. Attempts to capture adults were unsuccessful, but thirty-two foals were distributed among the zoos of Europe, two of them reaching the London Zoological Gardens.

Naturalists have studied them carefully and seem agreed that the Przewalski horse dates back to the prehistoric herds which roamed Europe before the Ice Age and were hunted for meat and hide. It is about twelve hands high, has a massive head with small ears, big teeth and heavy neck. Its colour is dun with black or brown dorsal stripe and legs. Its summer mane stands erect, its winter mane droops. Its most distinctive feature is a mealy muzzle.

Other European breeds have this unusual muzzle, but among British ponies it is peculiar to the Exmoor. The theory is that the Exmoor is a descendant of the wild horses of southern England which the Celts found when they crossed the sea from north-west Europe. They were being hunted by native tribes who were unaware that in the Middle East and Europe and parts of Asia the horse had become the most valuable animal known to man;

important for its speed and strength as well as for its meat and hide and bones and sinews.

The Celts trapped young horses and tamed them, riding them as hunters in pursuit of other animals or as war horses in tribal skirmishes. By the Iron Age the horse was venerated as essential to the survival of man. The Celtic goddess of fertility was Epona, the 'lady of the foals'. The first carving of a white horse on the chalk hills might have been an act of worship. Early chariots of the Britons were drawn by two, three or four small horses, galloping abreast. Those which Boadicea led against the Romans in the first century A.D. were drawn by such ponies with upright manes and pale muzzles, known to zoologists as the 'Celtic horse'.

One representative of the breed is confined now to that rugged corner of south-west England called Exmoor. For centuries, moorland families used it as a pack pony, carrying heavy burdens to mill and market. They used it also for hunting, which began as a necessity and became a sport. Towards the end of the nineteenth century, when education became compulsory and small schools were established in even the darkest corners like candles in the night, the family pony became the children's link with the world of books, trotting many miles along tracks too narrow and perilous for any vehicle. Thousands of years were in its moor-sense, its instinct for danger, its sure-footedness on steep descents. In a way the Exmoor family of the nineteenth century had as much cause as the Celts to venerate the little animal.

It was because of this history that I was interested by an Exmoor mare up for sale at six years old, ominously cheap and rumoured to be obstinate and vicious, as prone to kick as to bite, difficult to ride and almost impossible to catch. There were, however, other qualities which the gossips ignored; great depth of chest, enormous strength of back and ribs in the pack horse tradition, tough legs and hard feet, an essential boldness which neglect or stupidity had corrupted into arrogance. She promised to become a pony-and-a-half if we could succeed where others had failed.

We didn't know what to do; only what not to do. Punishment had plainly failed. So had shouting and running and offering bribes. We decided to turn her to a frugal paddock, so bare of grass that she could not glut herself. As companion we gave her a mild, kind chestnut which would come at the first call. Each day we called. The chestnut came and ate damp bran and pony nuts. The Exmoor remained at a distance, ears pricked and eyebrows lifted as she grazed. On the fifth day she jerked up her head when the chestnut moved towards us. You could see her thinking about it.

Punctuality was vital to this routine. We called at the same time, encouraging her to watch the gate and to listen for footsteps, to become as aware as the chestnut of what was about to happen. Each day she seemed a stride or two nearer, suggesting that curiosity and jealousy were beginning to overcome rejection. On the ninth day she ran up and down, still at a distance but plainly worried. On the twelfth she suddenly came, pounding to the gate in her determination to be caught first.

From that day we caught her punctually and handled her carefully, picking up her forefeet, then her hindfeet, leaning on her back, brushing her mane and tail. At the end of this routine she received whatever we had in a

pocket. She learned to stand and wait for it. Peppermint
was her favourite. She seemed not to realize that the
routine was being stealthily extended, that she was being
'kidded' into doing what previous owners had said she
would not do.

She was fitted with a snaffle bridle and ridden among
other ponies, always by the same boy who never carried
a stick. She seemed quite docile, making nonsense of her
reputation. We guessed what would happen when she
was ridden alone and out of sight from home. She turned
sly and 'clever', her ears flat and eyes sullen as she prepared to trigger her strength in rebellion. It was then the
boy had to be vigilant and patient, matching her determination with his own yet with good humour. By-
standers thought he would never make it. They offered
advice while he clung with his knees and coaxed and
grinned and refused to allow anyone to interfere.

But patience and good humour were not enough. We
needed something else and found it by accident. It was
music. The mare could be diverted by a pocket transistor; by 'Morning Service' or the Philharmonic or a
brass band. When the transistor faded or the B.B.C. insisted on talking, the boy sang and that was almost as
effective. He was ten years old and learning French and
when he sang 'The Marseillaise' she became the warhorse of Boadicea, striding towards the Romans with
comic truculence. In this way he got her to obey and to
enjoy obedience, acting a part in her way as he acted
another in his. While she was pretending to be the
'Celtic warhorse', he was pretending to be the champion
jockey and their developing partnership astonished
those who did not know about 'The Marseillaise'.

The achievement was in the means. We accepted it as further evidence that punishment is foolhardy because it is self-defeating, that the patient way can be the quickest. In less than three months the pony belonged to the boy and to nobody else, her head high and listening if he dared to be late from school. A pony's hearing is acute. She heard him coming long before we did.

Hunting proved her favourite game, her heart knocking in response to the huntsman's horn, her sawn-off legs pistoning a speed which bigger horses could not match for long. She found obvious glee in embarrassing them by attacking obstacles bigger than herself, throwing back a sneer at those which hesitated and looked for other ways.

Her reputation changed. The notorious rebel became the brave comedian, thundering out of a Thelwell cartoon to prove that among animals as among men, size is no measure of ability or courage. She became worth much more than I'd paid but of course there was no thought of selling; especially after an incident on the winter moor, when darkness came early from the granite tors, isolating mare and rider about twenty miles from home.

Through history men have been saved by their horses; the Cossack on the frozen wastes and the Bedouin in the blood-stained desert no less than the settler lost in the sage country of the Far West. It was to happen again on Dartmoor if only in miniature. My son was lost in a strange corner of the moor. He looked around at the silence and the bog cotton, at the darkness thickening on the hills. He did what he had been told. He dropped the reins and let the mare think it out.

The call of home is strong in all moorland breeds, even though home might be only the valleys where they were born. The Exmoor had inherited it, as well as an instinct for survival. Thousands of years were in her head as she chose a way around the bog cotton, then plodded towards the skyline; too wise to hurry or to take risks, nor worried by the cold, wet darkness which frightened the boy. It did not seem ridiculous that the pony which could still flinch from a paper bag should be full of courage now. Her stride quickened when she reached a track across the heather. She knew the track was going upward, that it had been made by sheep climbing to high ground at night. Moorland sheep would not take risks, so the track must be safe. She grunted as she climbed, seeming to be talking to herself about what she must do when she reached the granite ridge.

She passed along the ridge, looking for the best way down. The path she chose was diagonal. Her head was low as she peered for hidden boulders and sudden holes. When she reached a stream she looked for the place where the bank was broken, showing where wild ponies had crossed. Meanwhile the sky lifted and the world seemed bigger in the starlight. The boy hid his fingers in her mane, clinging to her warmth.

Other ponies heard her before I did. They raised their heads, their ears sharp. Racehorses came to their half doors, peering at the starlight and concentrating, then turning to prowl around the straw and come back and listen again. Their nuckering became excited. The kind chestnut, once the mare's companion and for long the victim of her bullying, sent a shrill neigh into the darkness. The Exmoor didn't answer, but her hoof-beats quickened, pattering like water down the valley.

I heard them then. I'd been at the gate a long time, watching the hill and imagining accident, vowing never to forgive her if she'd failed the boy. But when those sounds grew stronger, unmistakably the Exmoor coming boldly, as sure-footed in the dark as all her breed, gratitude flooded the holes of alarm and the vow became never to forget.

Racehorses wagged their heads. Other ponies nuckered and pawed their doors. But the Exmoor didn't want a heroine's welcome. She went by without a glance, making grumbling noises about boys who got lost and made her late. She smelled of rain and sweat and tiredness. When we took off bridle and saddle she butted aside congratulations and strode towards her field, seeking her favourite place, already brown and wet and flat. With a long groan she sank to a side and began to roll.

You can tell an animal's character by the way it rolls. Some turn around several times before lowering their bodies, betraying apprehension or diffidence. Others lie on one side and lurch their legs, then get up before preparing to roll on the other; contriving to seem polite, as though it would be indelicate to writhe and grunt or to expose their bellies. The Exmoor had no inhibitions. She rolled as vehemently as she did all else, her feet shadowboxing the stars before thumping over and resting and lurching back again. Only when she'd rolled enough did she rest a minute, sighing a confession down her nostrils. For two pins she'd have stayed down like the defeated.

That was enough. She struggled up and marched to the corner of the field where the grass was sweetest. It was all she needed. She dismissed warm mash and

sponge-downs and cleansing scrapers as so many
affectations. She wanted only grass and the stream and
to be left alone. It seemed typical.

For about seven years she was hunted regularly
carrying nine stones for six hours twice a week. When
the grass was poor or filled with rain she was given hay
and a few pony nuts but never corn. To give a moorland
pony corn is to risk inflaming temperament as well as
legs. Not once did she fall or think about quitting, although she was of no use at all in other sports.

Hunter trials, during which competitors jump alone
over a prepared course, exposed her limitations. She
would not jump straight or willingly without the stimu-
lus of hunting horn and hounds and other ponies. Her
boredom made trials seem a poor substitute for the real
thing. In her only gymkhana she disgraced herself;

completing one round of jumps with storming enthusiasm, then checking abruptly as she realized with astonishment that she was back where she had started. Apparently she was expected to go round and round, getting nowhere. It was an affront to her intelligence, to the love of a straight line which made her formidable as a hunter. She stalked out of the ring with a snort of disgust and was never asked to try again.

Now she's venerable and rotund with foal, bossing younger ponies and claiming a superior place in the hierarchy. She is at her best in winter, able to cope with cold more easily than with the breathless days of sunshine; but she looks best in summer, when her thick, tight coat shreds to a black shine like a forest pool. None could ever call her a pretty pony, but the qualities which are officially characteristic of the breed – strength and stamina, sharp intelligence and bottomless courage – are there in abundance and redeem her caprice.

You can make a partner of such a pony, as my sons did during their periods of growing up. They shared everything from camping holidays to ice cream; bite for bite, by all accounts, with the Exmoor getting the last as the cone-shaped biscuit crackled to a stump. She is in their boyhood and will not be forgotten.

5

THE VANNER

THEY brought your milk, your vegetables, bread and fish. If you lived in isolated corners, they brought paraffin and candles and hats for Sunday church. They were the 'vanners', trotting their daily routine with what amounted to punctuality in days when you guessed time by trains making smoke in the valley or by cows coming to the gate.

Every trader had his van and one or two vanners. If the rural round was long and steep, the horses worked alternate days and some customers would not buy if the wrong horse was between the shafts. These customers came to the gate with bread crusts and pieces of stale bun, feeding their favourite while talking with the driver who was also their gossipmonger and news-taster, sometimes their commentator on world affairs. The minutes of chat were as important as the transaction.

The experienced trader knew his horse was an advertisement, recognized before the name on the van, often better known than he was, more permanent than the driver who could be sacked for fiddling or asking for commission. Those traders who were shrewd as well as experienced understood that customers wanted more than whatever he had to sell, more even than the minutes of chat. They wanted to feel comfortable about the horse, especially in bad weather.

The shrewdest trader in my memory was a baker. He had several competitors yet he did the most trade, not because his bread was superior or offered in a greater variety of shapes, but because he equipped his horse with a rain sheet in winter and in summer with a straw hat which had tassels to keep off the flies. The hat had holes for the horse's ears and it didn't matter that the tassels were of little use. My elderly relatives were convinced this trader was a good baker because he was plainly a good man.

When a trader bought a horse, he was making a major investment which could subtly affect his business for more than a decade. If he chose wrongly and had to resell after a month or two, his customers were unsettled. If he bought a biter or kicker or one which flattened its ears in suspicion of strangers, his customers were nervous. If he got his values wrong and put appearance before all else, he might be lumbered with a flashy sham, prone to lameness at the end of the day.

The wise trader, made cautious by the experiences of his father and grandfather, gave a lot of time to the buying of a horse. He looked first at the feet, second at the legs. Only when he was sure that the feet were hard and well-shaped, the legs cold and firm and likely to stand years of steady work on rough roads, only then did he begin to consider the height and conformation, the eyes and ears as indications of temperament.

The ideal vanner was about fourteen hands high, with perfect feet and plenty of bone in its forelegs, amiable of eye and intelligent of ear, strong and determined yet not aggressive. As a bonus its colour was preferably distinctive, instantly recognizable from a distance so that none could confuse it with the horses of competitors. The price might be thirty-five pounds, although some traders paid more for a horse which could trot the final hill and come home with a flourish.

The vanner was never a breed. It was a type, like the cob and the hunter. In southern England hundreds of vanners came out of the New Forest; those windswept miles in Hampshire where horses have roamed for at least a thousand years. They proved popular for their hardiness and for their size, which at 14.2 hands is higher than any other southern moorland breed. Traders in Wales preferred the mountain cobs and ponies, while in East Anglia the humble vanner was often derived from the Norfolk Roadster, first of the trotting breeds and noble ancestor of the high-stepping Hackney which drew the carriages of the wealthy. North Country vans were drawn by the Fell or by its close neighbour the Dale, both of which graze regions of the Pennines. The reputation of the Fell for hardiness and steady diligence was established in the nineteenth century, when they were used as pack ponies to carry lead to the docks of Tyneside. Each carried sixteen stones in balanced panniers and needed to be capable of two hundred and forty miles a week.

In Scotland the most famous vanner was the Mainland, tallest of the Highland breeds and stronger than the ponies of Barra. On the Shetland Islands small carts were drawn by perky Shetlands, the strongest breed in the world in relation to its size.

For perhaps a hundred years the vanners kept trotting while our 'nation of shopkeepers' supplied 'courtesy with service', considering nothing too insignificant to be sold and delivered. A great-uncle of mine, who had a draper's shop in Pembroke, made a small fortune by delivering reels of cotton to women living so remote that they bought more than they needed, fearful that refusal would discourage his van from coming so far again.

He had two horses and they worked alternately. Both were mares, for he tended to believe, with the tribes of Arabia, that mares were the more loyal and dependable. He despised greys and mistrusted chestnuts with white legs; supposing white to be a sign of cowardice. He liked bays for their black legs and black feet, interpreting black as an indication of hardness. In his opinion yellow feet were 'as soft as butter'.

Working-class streets were sad when the horse-drawn van began to go out and the Trojan or Austin van began to come in. The first motor vans had hard tyres and horns with bulbs and brought smells of petrol and oil. Older customers were resentful, asking what had happened to the horses. Many traders, sensitive to the preju-

dices of their customers, did not immediately buy the
new means of transport. They waited for the old to decline into retirement, making frequent allusions to this
decline until even the most prejudiced pitied the old
horse and admitted change to be inevitable.

For more than ten years the horse-drawn mingled
with the motor-powered in the streets of our town, each
reluctant to concede right of way to the other yet the
driver of the horse-drawn always the winner of a show-
down, confident that he had the town on his side. The
town became increasingly sentimental about its horses as
their number declined, so that the last vanner seemed
more important than all the hundreds which had gone
before.

The last of the vanners which I remember was a bay
called Brownie. He knew the milk-round with such
authority that he needed no guidance, walking along
one side of the street while the roundsman poured milk
into jugs on the other. Brownie stopped at number
twenty-four in expectation of dried toast which made an
interesting noise when he crunched it, then crossed the
road to twenty-nine in the certainty of carrot, cut into
cubes and fed by the invalid who reached through a
ground floor window. If the arm was not long enough
Brownie mounted the pavement and inclined his head
through the lower half, peering into the smell peculiar to
a sick-room, his top lip groping around the white, thin
hand. Sundays were said to be bad days for the invalid,
because Brownie didn't come.

For about fourteen years Brownie made his rounds,
attended by a series of men who were less drivers than
male nurses, paid to make sure he got home all right. His

pace was slow and pensive, like a cricket umpire's. If number twenty-six was on holiday, which usually meant visiting a relative who was sick, he waited for the person next door to come out and explain, then to console his disappointment with something on account. When number forty-seven withdrew her custom, always inclined to take offence and nursing some grievance against the driver, Brownie continued to stop and wait, implying such incredulity that forty-seven relented. He must have been a great trial to his drivers, none of whom dared hustle him through all the years of stop and dawdle.

It was my task to take Brownie to his summer field when the daily stint was done. He needed no halter. You put a hand on his mane and spoke politely and hoped there would be no cars coming up the hill. Brownie could be pigheaded about cars when his work was done. All morning he had kept the wheels of his van in the left-hand gutter, never more than an inch from the pavement in accordance with the rules. But off duty it was different. He claimed the best of the road and walked down the middle like a North Country miner going for a pint; asserting a right which worried drivers coming up and delighted the old who shared his contempt of din and rattle and the smell of petrol.

Brownie was retired in the year of the Abdication but the working-class did not forget. During their ceremonial strolls on Sunday afternoons, they took bags of crusts to the field near the railway and Brownie came solemnly to the gate, still like a cricket umpire coming out for the second innings yet seeming younger without his bridle. They said it was the absence of blinkers, enabling them to see his eyes. Brownie's eyes were the colour of bumble bees. He did best during the week of the Coronation, when the working-class celebrated with street-teas. What the young couldn't eat was borne in baskets to his gateway.

One of the reasons why they made such a fuss of old Brownie was the fear that the last of the vanners would prove the end of working horses in a world dominated by machines. Pessimists predicted that horses would be soon confined to racehorses, hunters and polo ponies. They were proved wrong as pessimists often are.

A generation born during the 1939–45 war had little cause to be excited by machines. They took for granted what had seemed remarkable or frightening innovations. To the astonishment of pessimists and the consternation of those blacksmiths and saddlers who had put up shutters in expectation of famine, they wanted ponies, the working-class breeds which had roamed the wild lands for centuries and were cheap to buy and to keep. Riding, which had been the accomplishment of the few, became the sport of the many.

Suddenly the New Forest was popular as a hunter. Welsh ponies proved bold and nimble in gymkhanas. Fell ponies became favourites of families in the north, passing from the eldest through sons and daughters to the youngest. Fathers bought Shetlands as first ponies for children almost too young to walk. The horse was saved by the young to the delight of older generations who somehow contrived to pay.

It is an astonishing rejuvenation, not confined to Britain yet seeming to be British in its feeling for the past. It seems to me that the past is in the merriment of hooves. You can hear pack ponies carrying tin and lead and fleeces; the dreaded Dragoons hunting enemies of the King; half-see smugglers' ponies coming from the shingle with 'whisky for the parson, brandy for the clerk'. It's an exciting sound, like history come alive. One way of knowing history is to know about your horse.

6

STAGE AND MAIL

YOU go down a step to the passage of the London Inn.
The passage is stone-flagged and the beams are low.
There are coach horns on the walls and pieces of harness
and prints of how it used to be, if only in the imaginations of artists who liked to paint fat grins and
checked waistcoats and serving wenches with cheeks like
apple blossom.

On the left is the dining-room, where coach passengers were served in half an hour while the kitchen
sweated and servants ran and the turn-spit terrier
panted in its cage. Beyond it is the small room called 'the
snug', where men met to whisper news from London or

the Channel ports. On the right is the bar where people of the town gathered to listen and watch, tuned-in to the rumours which the travellers brought.

At the back of the inn, shut in now by other buildings but open then to the sun and stars, is the cobbled yard where teams were changed. Ostlers lead away the spent, while youths pumped water to the troughs and the coachman drank hot ale and small boys of the town crept from their corners to watch with awe, for this coach was 'The Flier', acknowledged to be the fastest, this driver the famous Coachey who was never late.

Coachey leaned near the window of the kitchen, never taking his eyes from what the yard staff were doing yet enjoying the admiration of the kitchen maids. Ostlers were harnessing the new team. They could do it in fifty seconds, but there was no haste now for the passengers were dining and would not come out until the warning gong. Coachey watched them carefully for there were dark miles ahead and broken roads and deep fords and lives could be lost by a broken trace. When the team was ready with youths holding the heads of the leaders and the wheelers chiming their bits, Coachey moved from the window to inspect, beginning on the off side, behind the wheel-horse, and passing around the coach, looking up to the luggage and down to the wheels, checking whatever might be loose or perilous.

He came up the near side, making sure his whip was placed ceremonially across the backs of the wheelers, that the horses were sound and would last two hours. He checked the reins, especially the buckles which attached them to the bits, implying an indifference which made others nervous and respectful, anxious to be in their

places before the great man was ready. Coachey took
the near lead rein in his left hand and lowered the hand
until the rein was taut against his hip. He tightened the
off lead rein with similar precision, then took up the
wheel reins, middling them between the fingers of his
right hand and swinging the ends over an arm. He was
meticulous about this. He knew he was being watched.

The yard was silent as he took the whip from the
backs of the wheelers and put his left foot on a wheel
hub, his right on the roller bolt, swinging up with his left
foot moving to a step, his right to the footboard. When
he reached his box he arranged the longest of his several
coats, covering his legs with a driving apron to give
further protection from wind and rain. He passed the
reins to his left hand, adjusted his whip and glanced a
final check. His left hand relaxed slightly. The horses
leaned to their collars. For a moment they stood with
traces taut. The ostlers waited. Faces in the yard held
their breaths.

On the stroke of time Coachey nodded; the ostlers
stood back and the faces cheered while the passengers
lurched and small boys vowed to be like Coachey when
they were old enough. A moment later the coach was in
the street and the passengers were swaying while the
horses settled to the canter which was the only pace
Coachey allowed. He was twenty-one miles from the
next stage. He would be there in one hour, fifty-nine
minutes and ten seconds, allowing fifty seconds for the
change. That was his time-table and the time-table was
his boss.

Small boys pursued the coach out of town and men
stopped their work to see it go while women came to

their windows, excited by the noise, by the glimpse of nameless faces hurrying towards the unknown. But not all the windows had excited faces. Some were blank, for the faces had drawn back in distress.

The working span of horses on the fast routes was only three years. They were compelled to the same pace regardless of hills and heavy luggage, of mud and floods and ice and snow. Those which fell and scarred their knees were used on the night runs, beside the blind and the deaf and broken-mouthed. They ran until they dropped. Coachmen called them 'cattle'.

An ancestor of mine was among those who drew back from their windows when the coach horn sounded, frightened and bewildered because there seemed nothing they could do to save the horses. The churches were silent; the Church of England fearful of offending the rich who were its patrons, the Roman Catholics adamant that horses were 'chattels' and any preaching of pity 'a pestilent heresy'. Only Methodists were angry and unafraid.

My ancestor was not a Methodist. She was an individualist, sure there was something she could do and doing it persistently, despite the embarrassment of her family. She came to the yard of the London Inn with bread crusts for the spent teams. When there were no crusts, she brought shreds of grass and held them out while ostlers laughed and her son, who was a trader in the town and almost a church-warden, fretted and apologized and explained how old she was. On market days she brought grass to cows which had been left enclosed or tethered. When ponies were impounded as strays, she brought them water because someone had

told her that none was fed or watered until its ownership
was proved.

All the time she was afraid; afraid of the jeering faces,
of being kicked or bitten, of being discovered by her
eldest son. She was frightened most on the eve of fair
days, when strangers came to town, driving herds of wild
ponies to the field called Sanctuary near the church.
Nooses were looped around their necks and tethered to
trees and bushes. During the night they struggled and
the slip knots tightened. Some were strangled. A few
broke their necks. Most were still alive in the morning,
exhausted by their struggling and ready to be sold as
broken. My ancestor wanted her son to go there in the
night and cut the ropes and set the ponies free, but of
course her son would not.

She supposed she was alone in distress. Unable to
read, she could not know that in other parts of England
powerful men were trying to introduce laws which
would protect animals from abuse. I doubt that she ever
knew about those who met at Liverpool in 1808 to celebrate a royal anniversary. What could have been just
another social occasion, made mellow by brandy and
cigars and genial banter, became the origin of the
Society for Preventing Cruelty to Brute Animals, the
first to be formed in the world.

Its members campaigned by letters and by speeches,
but individual eloquence was not enough. Lord Erskine,
a Scot and former Lord Chancellor, tried to introduce a
Bill which would forbid ruthless punishment of coach
horses in races against the clock or between rival
companies. The attempt failed, partly because of criti-
cism aimed by William Windham, who asked on whom

guilt could be focused: the coachman, the owners, or passengers who insisted that punctuality was an element of the contract? In 1816 the Attorney-General, Sir William Garrow, introduced a Bill designed to protect horses from 'enormous abuses', but this was also lost because Members of the House of Lords doubted that any two persons could agree on what constituted cruelty.

Meanwhile, the brutalities of fair days continued, and competition between coach companies became more reckless. A new company touted for passengers by promising to return fares if the coach was a minute late. It was on this route that a coachman broke three whips in six hours, that fifteen horses died in a week.

None seemed big enough to fight the madness until Richard Martin, the wealthy Member for Galway, stood up in the House of Commons to earn the derisive nickname 'Humanity' Martin. He was larger than life as a reformer needs to be; passionate and garrulous, likely to take a blunderbuss to any who dared trespass on his acres, a duelling pistol to whoever wounded his honour. Minor Members, listening to him introducing his 'Ill-treatment of Horses Bill', were intimidated by his manner and respectful of his wealth, bewildered that one who owned two hundred thousand acres and was a despot among his tenants could risk ridicule in such a cause. His first attempts were unsuccessful. Members could not take him seriously. But Richard Martin persisted until his reception in the House of Commons mellowed to a kind tolerance. In 1822 Members found themselves supporting proposals which a few years before would have seemed ridiculous.

On 22nd June of that year it became an offence to

'beat, abuse or ill-treat any horse, mare, gelding, mule, ass, ox, cow, heifer, steer, sheep or other cattle'. There was no plea for dogs, cats or birds.

If she had known about it my ancestor would have clasped her hands in gratitude, supposing that the law would be immediately effective. But it is easier to introduce a law than to implement it. Witnesses were reluctant to give evidence; nervous of their neighbours, of their priests, of being branded cranks or sentimentalists. When they were brave enough and the evidence was overwhelming, magistrates were reluctant to inflict the maximum sentence of two months' imprisonment. Stage coach drivers were fined the minimum penalty of ten shillings and left the court like heroes, confident that the fine would be paid by their employers. Carters pleaded guilty only to obeying orders, while owners of post horses disclaimed responsibility for what happened to their horses during periods of hire. The shrewd among the working-class wondered why the coachmen of the rich were apparently beyond the law.

Within a year the historic Bill was being treated with contempt. Martin realized it and in 1824 gave active support to a society which included Members of Parliament and clergymen. The Rev. Arthur Broome, vicar of St Mary's, Bromley-le-Bow, was the first Secretary. It called itself the Society for the Prevention of Cruelty to Animals, but it did not receive the 'Royal' prefix until 1840. For sixteen years its influence was limited. The windows of our town saw no change in the conduct of fair days, no mercy for coach horses or for those which could be hired.

My ancestor must have despaired. She had never

heard of humanitarianism or philobrutism or zoophily
or Rousseauism or any of the fine words which speech-
makers used. She didn't know that the process of reform
had begun; that the guilty would soon be afraid more of
those who watched than of the law. She heard only the
sounds outside. In the night she heard the mail coach.

The mail coach service was introduced by John
Palmer in 1784 to take the place of 'post boys', who were
not boys as stable lads are not lads. They were men with
leather faces, their mouths obscured by mufflers to keep
out wind and dust, their hats tilted down to protect their
eyes. They rode local breeds of ponies at little more than
five miles an hour, accused often of loitering and sus-
pected of intrigues with highwaymen on the moonlit
roads. Riding in relays they brought the mail from
London to Bath in about fifty hours. John Palmer promised that fifteen would be enough.

His first mail coach weighed eighteen hundred-
weights, was smaller than the stage and carried four
passengers, all of them inside. Only the coachman and
guard rode outside. The guard carried a blunderbuss
and a brace of pistols and was equipped with a timepiece
in a sealed box, with a horn to warn towns and toll gates
that the mail was coming. The first run from London to
Bath, using teams of four at intervals of ten miles,
fulfilled Palmer's prediction. The Postmaster-General
sanctioned rapid expansion of the service; subsidizing
inns with the proviso that they could not be used by stage
coaches; encouraging the purchase of thousands of
horses and the construction of hundreds of coaches. On
the London to Edinburgh route alone, the Post Office
used ten coaches and 620 horses, with more than twenty

inns pledged to serve passengers and to give the mails rapid distribution.

Mail was distributed locally by the post boys who were jealous and disgruntled, considering themselves relegated to a minor role. They rode their ponies to scattered villages and hamlets, collecting mail as well as delivering it. Once a week their bags were heavy with newspapers and magazines from London.

Officially they were the finger-tips of the service, but the post boy who rode out of our town, wrapped in coats and mufflers, did not go beyond the crossroads near the moor. He was met there by Grannie who seemed to have no other name. She came from the shelter of a moorland wall and reached for what the post boy brought, hiding it at once beneath her shawl. They never spoke. They were supposed to hate each other, yet both belonged to the old way and were determined to preserve it.

Grannie took the mail to a house on the hill, where the daughter could read and could give a name to each package. Grannie's memory was good. She had several pockets in her skirt and put a package into each, telling herself which was for the parsonage and which for the home farm and which for the Traveller's Rest. She was not paid. Each recipient gave her something; silver or eggs or perhaps a meal. Once a week she was made wealthy by newspapers and magazines and out of this wealth she saved enough for the bad days, when she waited at the crossroads for hooves which did not come.

In the mid-nineteenth century the last horse-drawn 'Royal Mail' came west from London and flags were lowered to half-mast. The tradition of speed and punctuality passed to the Great Western Railway, which also

adopted the naming of engines, making them as individual as coaches had been. But the post boy was still
needed, ironically surviving the coachman and guard
who had humiliated him. Branch-lines had not yet
linked villages with railway towns and even when the
links were complete, there were remote places which no
vehicle could reach or any stranger find.

In the 1960s, eighty years after Grannie disappeared
from the crossroads, mail was still being delivered by
pony and rider on the southern hills of Dartmoor. The
rider wore no uniform. Wrapped in heavy coats he was a
hunched figure on his dark-brown pony, coming out of
the mist as though from another century.

7

WORKING IN PAIRS

THEY had difficulty getting it down the stairs. It was
long and heavy and the stairs bent sharply like an arm.
Those in front panted orders to those behind, their
voices hushed because this was the coffin and the mourners were listening and the hearse was at the door.

The man who was suddenly a coffin had been a horseman. Framed photographs of horses were on the walls of
his kitchen and the foot of a favourite horse was his
favourite ornament. His last request had been for an old-
fashioned funeral. No motor hearse with cars following;

but black horses with black plumes and the coachman
wearing black gloves.

They gave him what he wanted. It was the last horse-
drawn funeral to be seen by our town and what I remember is the slowness of the horses, their natural gaiety
subdued, their eyes down in what seemed to be deference. They'd known what would be required of them
as soon as they'd seen the black plumes, the black crepe
on the bridles. You couldn't recognize them as the pair
which also drew the fire engine.

The fire engine was owned by the town and staffed by
volunteers who wore helmets which shone like the brass
instruments in the town band. It was kept in a shed near
the market and the volunteers were summoned by the
ringing of tenor and treble bells. Everyone recognized
the peculiar dong-ding from the church tower and the
wives of volunteers were supposed to sleep lightly so that
they could awaken the heroes and find their uniforms,
sometimes helping with the buttons or finding the
hatchet. Our brigade was proud of its speed of turn-
out.

Seven volunteers ran to the shed which was called the
fire station, while the eighth ran to the mews where the
horses were stabled. The undertaker lived above the
stables. The volunteer found him fumbling his braces
and panting questions, frightened by the bells bouncing
their sounds across the roofs.

The horses came out with eyes wild and nostrils
flaring, catching the sounds of running, perhaps the
smell of smoke. The undertaker ran behind them to the
fire station, holding the long reins and almost stepping
on the traces. Half the town helped to back them and

fasten them, to hold the doors wide as the undertaker became the fire engine driver and clambered to his perch. Someone clanged the bell. The horses leapt and the volunteers clung, thinking ten miles an hour fast as the vehicle swung out of the market square towards the red stain in the sky.

Sometimes the fire was a barn ten miles away, and when the engine got there the volunteers were frustrated because the hoses were not long enough or the stream deep enough. Often the horses did not come back till morning, when they ceased to be fire horses and became carriage horses, booked to meet the train from Paddington and to convey guests to the town's best hotel.

One of this pair was a former steeplechaser, which had almost run in the Grand National of 1922. He had damaged his forelegs in a preliminary race and been retired from racing, a virtual cripple until the undertaker of our town bought him cheaply and kept him trotting the roads. Men used to say, as they watched the carriage pass, that this horse might be fully restored by steady trotting, might even race again and bring honour to the town. It wasn't as implausible as it sounded, for the American-bred Rubio had won the Grand National of 1908 after breaking down more than three years before. In those years Rubio had drawn the hotel bus from the railway station at Towcester to the Prospect Arms and back again, earning his keep while trotting hardness into his legs. We schoolboys looked ahead to it happening again, but it did not. Perhaps our horse was not good enough. More probably he was too old.

Another pair of horses drew the carrier's cart which

T–C

was the only link that isolated villages had with the market town. The cart was heavy and the passengers sat on either side, facing each other with baskets and hampers, perhaps with a calf half-trussed by sacking in the space between their knees. They began the journey with excited small talk, for the journey to market was a big event and there was always plenty to tell. But the talk frayed away as the horses plodded and the big wheels rumbled. Heads became heavy and drooped like flowers, jolting awake when the wagon stopped at a wayside cottage and new voices approached. Six miles an hour was considered fair. Men got out on the hills and an iron shoe braked a wheel during steep descents.

The horses had broad backs, and bells on their harness, and were known to passengers by their names. Bella and Daisy worked together for twenty years, as famous locally as a music-hall act. They served the villages which branchline railways neglected and were still the only means of public transport when the first bus crept nervously towards the hills in the early 1920s.

Some of the best horses in the neighbourhood were bought by hauliers for the regular transport of bulk supplies to and from factories; for the hauling of trucks along railway sidings to piers where ships were loading. The best hauliers had great, dappled Percherons, originally bred by farmers in the Le Perche district of France and regarded with awe like heavyweight boxers. Women called them the 'Gentle Giants'. The man who drove and cared for them, as dedicated as a priest, loved them for their willingness, their nobility and – not least – for their clean legs.

Percherons have no long hair (or feather) around

their lower legs, so the evening task of cleaning was
made simpler for the Percheron man than for the
Clydesdale man, who loved his Clydesdale and would
admit no fault in them, yet whose working day was
made longer by the need to clean the long, white hair on
each leg and foot. This was no easy task in winter, when
Clydesdales had been hauling through mud. There was
a saying among other horsemen that you needed to be a
saint to work with Clydesdales and like it.

Another haulier preferred the Suffolk Punch, bred in
East Anglia since 1506 and famous for its strength in a
direct pull. People came to the pavements to watch our
pair of chestnut Punches working with a kind of furious
majesty, their ears sharp for the voice which walked
beside them when the hill was cruel. Good horsemen
used their voices to encourage, then to call for more
during the final yards; like the pack leader of rugby
forwards when they push over for a try. Such horsemen
scorned the use of whips and sometimes the use of reins.
Towns were proud of those who walked yards away,
calling instructions with the certainty that the horses
would not miss a word.

The wise haulier, having invested in the best, super-
vised their feeding with fanatical care. Eighteen pounds
of oats a day were not unusual, the grain slightly crushed
by hand-machine to assist the process of mastication,
perhaps dampened as well to make mastication easier.
Some horsemen, catching the fanaticism of their employers, used eggs to dampen, robbing their own hen-
houses despite the protests of their wives. Six eggs a day
were not too many. Bantam eggs were considered as
nutritious as hen eggs. One horseman kept hens and

bantams for no other purpose. I remember his son saying that his family never had eggs for breakfast.

Hay had to be old yet sweet, without dust when you shook it. Hauliers differed most in their choice of hay, but all were agreed that meadow hay could not be hard enough. Mixtures of rye grass and red clover gave the right hard muscle shine. It was fed from the rack or chopped into chaff. It also supplied the essential roughage and, because of its importance to the teams, the hay harvest was crucial to the haulier as well as to farmers in the neighbourhood.

Oats and hay were the basic foods but some hauliers added supplementaries, including black treacle and chopped carrots and watercress and fish oils. The one I knew best was cranky about dandelions, insisting they were not only a source of iron but a delicacy which stabled horses greeted with delight.

It was true. Their nostrils trembled when you came in with the green stuff, their natural courtesy suspended as they nudged and fussed, grudging the time necessary to chop the roots and shred the leaves, to break the stems and expose the juices. I didn't know then that this haulier had borrowed his crankiness from stonecutters in the long ago who had dug dandelions from the hedgerows to supplement their bread and cheese, biting the roots as a substitute for radish and getting accustomed to the hot sting.

He also believed that everything which horses needed could be found in hedgerows if you had gypsy eyes and knew where to look. He encouraged me to gather blackberry leaves, regardless of fingers sore from prickles; nut leaves when they were young and green, before autumn

began to toughen them; fat thistles with the juices
dribbling. It shocked me that horses which had the best
could take thistles delicately into their mouths and
squeeze out the juices with delight reflected in their eyes.
I'd supposed thistles to be tramp food, suitable only for
donkeys.

Not all hauliers could afford the best horses; not all
mills and factories would pay the fees which the best
hauliers needed to charge. Minor hauliers bought cheap
horses and fed them poorly, reducing costs in order to
keep prices low. This was considered good business
during the bleak years of the late 1920s, when the plight
of overworked horses seemed less urgent than the plight
of families whose fathers were unemployed. But occasionally the conscience of the town was stricken by the
ugly spectacle of horses struggling, going to their knees
in a kind of entreaty as their back feet slipped and the
wheels slid while the driver used the whip with the
cruelty of panic, appalled by what would happen if the
wagon slid further or the load toppled.

The town knew it wasn't the driver's fault; that he
would lose his job if he begged for smaller loads or more
time or for an extra horse on the steep hills. Yet spec-
tators focused their anger on him because they were not
sure who else to blame. Occasionally the incident was
reported and the driver and haulier appeared before
magistrates, some of whom were also mill owners and
factory owners, vitally interested in keeping prices
down. Perhaps their indignation was assumed. Perhaps
it was genuine, as though to sit on a Bench is to acquire
another identity. But everyone knew that the driver and
haulier were not alone in guilt. Any sentence could be

only a partial justice and the wisest constable of our town knew it.

He didn't bother with note-book and pencil. He un-hooked the wooden block from the back of the wagon and wedged it beneath a wheel; holding the weight for a time, giving the horses partial respite in the hope that, with all the men coming from the pavements to lend their strengths and himself taking the lead horse from the frightened driver, he could get the wagon climbing and the life of the town moving. This constable was never promoted, perhaps because he did not keep his note-book full; but he was respected in our town, not least by those who liked horses.

There was another pair which appeared occasionally, drawing a long, low vehicle like a bathchair and driven

by a lady whose legs were always wrapped in rugs. But
we didn't take this pair seriously, for they were donkeys,
at the bottom of the class in schoolboy language, their
ears flopping like a jester's cap, their eyes slanted and
inscrutable like Chinese. We believed donkeys to be
peasant animals and couldn't understand why a lady
preferred them to horses. Our parents couldn't understand it either. They implied that such perversity was
permissible only because the lady was rich, so we had to
mind our manners and keep straight faces when the
penny-sized hooves trotted by.

I wish now that I'd taken these donkeys seriously and
had scraped acquaintance with the lady whose legs were
always hidden. She might have had much to tell about
their intelligence, their capacity for affection which can
be as loyal as a dog's. In another way donkeys are like
cats, inclined to consider what you want, then to decide
if it is worth doing. If it isn't, their obstinacy can be
humiliating; which is why experienced horsemen used
to say that if you can drive a donkey, you can drive
anything. Presumably the lady in the grey hat could
have driven anything, for she handled her donkeys with
ease.

They were a Jack and Jenny. The Jack was darker
and slightly taller but the Jenny was boss, which seemed
right to women watching from the pavement. The pair
made three stops in our long High Street: at the pastry
cook's, where the proprietor came out with a cardboard
box which set young imaginations wondering; at the
book shop, where the pages of *The Strand* magazine
smelled as new as varnish; and at the bank on the corner,
which had pillars like a temple and a kind of hush. At no

time did the driver get out. She was met by senior assistants whose deference made it plain that she was rich enough to be important. I think they were embarrassed by the donkeys.

But an old man of the town was wiser. He called them the 'Jesus pair' and at once I saw Jerusalem and the cheering faces of Palm Sunday, when Christ rode the humblest of animals towards the shadow of the Cross. I think the lady knew what the old man called them, for occasionally their glances met in a smile of understanding.

8

THE HORSE FAIR

ONCE a year a white glove welcomed you to our town. It was attached to a decorated pole and extended from one of the gabled buildings at what used to be the town gate. It was supposed to be a gesture of hospitality. Hawkers and farmers recognized it as a promise that for twenty-four hours tolls and licensing restrictions would be suspended. The day was the May fair; held in the market square where the inns were several and where upper windows gave the families of traders a remote yet privileged view.

The day began early, when the dew was still wet and
the fields were smoking and the sounds of hooves coming
from villages and gypsy camps were as loud as footsteps
in church. By eight, when the shops began to take down
their shutters and to raise their blinds like the lids of
broody hens awakening, there were perhaps a hundred
horses; old horses and young, drays and vanners, all with
rope or webbing halters, tethered to the walls of the
Wesleyan chapel on one side, the courtyard of an inn on
the other. Some were tied three to a ring, their heads
drawn close like conspirators.

They were divided into groups; vanners in one group,
dray horses in another, miscellaneous cobs and ponies in
a huddle near the steps of the chapel. The least favour-
able place, where the wall was low and the midday
shade promised to be narrow, was given to old horses
with broken feet and stump tails and pits above their
eyes. You didn't need to look at their teeth to guess
their ages. Those pits were hint enough. No one had
bothered to plait their manes or to tie their tails with
raffia. They were here for one purpose and everyone
knew it yet did not talk about it; for old years are sad
years and the women of our town, coming to watch with
hands tucked beneath their aprons and their eyes as
quick as birds, did not want to think about what would
happen when the bargaining was over and the shunting-
engine brought the horse trucks. If they were lucky these
old horses would be slaughtered soon; their meat sold to
kennels and zoos, their fat to factories for the making of
soap, their hides for the lining of shoes and boots, their
feet for glue, their manes and tails for the stuffing of
mattresses. If they were unlucky they would be worked

more weeks or months until they were drained; finally passing to the knacker, who was ugly in the imaginations of the women, splattered by horses' blood which was subtly different from cattle blood. The women were revolted.

Gypsies had the longest wall, conceded to them by the nervous withdrawal of others who had come to sell. You could tell the gypsy at a glance. He was as brown as the earth, his hair black and ragged like a bird in the wind. He wore a neckerchief, tied in a knot at the side of his neck, and his hands were like leather and the small rings in his ears gave him a pirate look. I was nervous of his eyes. They were never looking when you were looking. They were hooded.

My grandfather's suspicion of gypsies was confused by respect. He would not buy from them because they were unscrupulous and knew more than he did about horses. Yet often he was tempted, for they brought good horses to the fair and knew how to display them in long trots across the cobbles. I suspect that he would have liked to risk his skill against them and to emerge with a bargain, which would have given him something to boast about; but caution kept his sovereigns in his purse. He bought from other farmers who spoke his language or from dealers who dared no blatant trickery lest he exaggerate their infamy and disgrace them.

But more than inherited caution and respect were at the back of my mind as I watched the gypsies. I'd inherited also my mother's apprehensive contempt, supposing them to be not only clever and sly but cruel, masking their cruelty so that it could not be detected. She had heard of gypsies concealing a horse's lameness by deliberately laming the opposite leg, compelling the horse to share its weight evenly. She'd heard of ash leaves and black treacle, mixed in a potion which Christians could not imitate although they doubtless tried. Since every gypsy was a shoeing smith and knew a horse's foot as though he could see through the wall to the three bones and the tender sole, every gypsy hoof was suspect. Clever shoeing could hide defects. Unscrupulous shoeing could inflict calculated pain, so that a horse pranced in a travesty of eagerness.

The wise trader, seeking a vanner, would not buy a gypsy horse until all its shoes were removed and the feet exposed. He felt them for heat, since each foot is filled with blood and inflammation can glow in the hard horn, then gestured for the horse to be trotted on the roughest cobbles, aware that trotting is the most revealing pace and that cobbles are the most demanding surface.

When the trader was sure of the feet, he examined legs and teeth, examining both jaws because the upper teeth are less easily faked than the lower. If the horse was a male and supposed to be four years old, he looked for the early tushes; those cone-shaped teeth which begin to appear at four and have no apparent function, except as a means of self-defence. If the age was supposed to be six or seven, he looked for the black marks called 'beans'; but still he could not be sure, for gypsies were supposed to be clever at 'bishoping', which was my grandfather's ugly word for faking black marks with hot wires.

If he gave the gypsy the benefit of any doubt about the teeth, he checked height by hand and eye, knowing what his van required and that an inch could make a difference. He did not do this until the animal had been led to flat tarmac, well aware that a gypsy could add an inch to a horse by standing it on sloping ground. He measured from the top of the wither, the fingers of his right hand closed, the thumb forgotten. Each finger was an inch and four fingers were a 'hand', so that a horse of fourteen hands was fifty-six inches high. But if you watched closely you guessed that he had a more personal, perhaps more reliable, method; assessing height by the top button of his waistcoat, which he knew from previous purchases to be fourteen hands high.

Bargaining was a private duel between gypsy and trader, with no auctioneer to stimulate bids, no veterinary surgeon to give advice. The asking figure was always high, the first offer always low. Gradually the figures approached each other like gunmen in a Western film. Often the haggling took two hours, the trader moving away and inspecting other horses before drifting back to assess what delay had done to the gypsy's nerve. Sometimes the trader miscalculated and the gypsy got his price from one less experienced. Often the deal was suddenly concluded with an exchange of money; the trader paying cash, the gypsy returning the traditional 'luck' money which was the equivalent of a discount. There was supposed to be a ceremonial handshake, but few traders would shake hands with gypsies.

The trader took the horse and was surrounded by those who could be trusted to admire his choice. After a few minutes of admiration and congratulation, he beckoned the van driver who would assume responsibility for it and would drive it for all the town to see. The employee led the horse towards the stable, nervous of it because you could never be confident of gypsy horses

when another hand first touched them, yet proud like a
school pupil walking off with a prize. The trader
watched them go, joking about how much it had cost,
more than he could afford because times were hard and
credit slates full and even the gentry were slow to pay;
but none of his friends believed the lament as they passed
towards the nearest inn, where he became a hero of the
crowded bar. He had proved his opulence and backed
his judgment and those who could do neither were generous in their flattery.

Morning hours were for buying and selling. Afternoon hours were for drinking and gambling, for sending
shouts of laughter through opened windows while the
landlord's wife carved cold beef in further proof of hospitality and beggars played tin whistles and the town
idiot gave his customary response to the taunt that he
could not lift ten stones. He weighed ten stones, so the
taunting faces placed a basket on the floor and demanded that he crouch in it and seize the handles and
lift himself. They promised gold if he succeeded, so the
poor idiot crouched and heaved and wept in bewilderment and frustration. You could tell by the laughter in which inn the idiot was performing.

Women came to the square in the afternoon, moving
among the muddled stalls, grimacing at the prices and
mourning the decline in quality, occasionally reaching
to the deep pocket of their skirts and bringing out their
purses. The stalls had striped canopies, red and white
like peppermint sticks, and what they offered were
goods traditional to fair day; toffee apples and gingerbread and nougat, all sticky and sweet and declared by
my mother to be a wicked waste as well as bad for your

teeth. My favourite stall smelled of harness and invited your imagination to invent horses for the collars and breeching, to put faces into the bridles. The faces of my invention were always chestnuts with white blazes.

The stall beside it offered shopping baskets which creaked when you lifted them and wicker chairs which creaked when you sat in them. One basket dominated all others. It was long as a woman's arms could span, officially a laundry basket but called a 'clothes basket' by my mother whose wash day was Monday and who yearned for a basket so majestic. The man behind this stall was pale and blind. He identified people by their voices. Wealthy ladies, who wore tweeds and heavy shoes and shapeless hats, came from the Georgian houses to buy his baskets, admiring them because they were handmade. I watched them count silver into his palm. His touch was supposed to be hyper-sensitive, immediately identifying the halfcrown among the florins.

The grand ladies passed to a neighbouring stall, where a woman in a white apron, severely starched to match the false cuffs on her wrists, sold cream so thick you needed a knife to cut it and of a colour so deep you'd think the sun had looked into the huge, brown bowls, to leave its reflection in them. My mother approved this cream because it had been made 'in the proper manner' by straining milk into shallow pans each containing half a pint of water, by leaving it for twenty-four hours and then scalding over wood fires before leaving it again for from twelve to thirty-six hours, the final period varying with the weather. Sullen weather, grumbling with unheard thunder, was as bad for the cream-makers as for the butter-girls.

By early evening it was almost over. Gypsies had passed unnoticed through the crowd, returning to their notorious camps where women made brooms and artificial flowers. Farmers were staggering to their traps, each trusting his horse to know where home was. The town policeman lifted a farmer who couldn't find the step and hoisted him to the seat, unbuckling the reins and tying him there when his body lolled like Guy Fawkes on a bonfire. The constable spoke to the horse and the trap moved away. Fair day always ended in drunkenness, to the disgust of traders who became Methodists and Wesleyans and Congregationalists and Rechabites as soon as their shops were closed.

The last fair was held in 1938, but only a few horses came. There was no white glove, no stall smelling of leather, no sunshine bowls of cream, no blind man selling baskets. Only one stall persisted. It offered nougat and gingerbread and toffee apples and the wasps still hovered around this stall as they had in what my parents called the 'old days', when there'd been too many horses for the sale rings and boys had been paid halfpennies to hold them in side streets. The only other custom to remain was the extension of licensing hours, so that inns remained open all day and the same farmer, much older now and heavier, was hoisted to his trap at the end of it. The horse was different but its instinct for home was the same.

Each autumn there was also a pony fair, to which animals were driven from the moor: mares with their foals trotting close; young colts, frightened yet truculent, kicking at those who chased them with sticks. Half the boys were armed with sticks for the pony fair.

For more than a thousand years ponies have roamed Dartmoor. They were described as 'wild horses' in documents of the eleventh century and are still wild in that they roam more than two hundred square miles of heather and bracken and are never confined or brought to shelter. But all are owned and have brands. They are the property of hill farmers who have inherited or purchased rights of grazing on common land. Once a year the ponies are rounded up in the traditional 'drift', which used to be a great day for moorland families, especially for the young. They were summoned by a horn, sounded from the highest hill; and the drift became a meeting of cousins and second cousins, of friends who had new gossip and old jokes to tell. Dartmoor families of the nineteenth century had to make their own fun. The drift was the best day of their year, especially if the summer had been good, with frequent rain to keep the grass new. The ponies were fat and foals were strong and had not wandered far in their search for grazing.

They were driven to the biggest farmyard in the vicinity and segregated, each farmer recognizing his brand and selecting those brood mares which were needed to produce foals next May. Most of the young colts were surplus and were brought to the fair, where prices varied but ten shillings for a foal was considered good.

Dartmoors were used as pack ponies until the late nineteenth century, for the first road was not begun until 1772 and long after that the wilderness remained so wild and perilous that only the native pony could be trusted to cross it safely. When the need for pack ponies declined, mine owners of Wales and Derbyshire needed

T–D

ponies to take the places of women and children underground. The ponies had to be small yet sturdy. Above all
they had to be cheap. Agents bought on behalf of mine
owners, buying more than they needed because not all
would survive the journey or be fit for work on arrival.

Before a network of railways linked the West Country
with the mining areas, ponies were driven three hundred
miles or more, for part of the way following the tracks of
cattle being driven to Smithfield market. The cattle arrived haggard and masked with dust; so did the ponies,
which mattered less because they had cost less. What
happened to them on the way, when they were at the
mercy of the stupid and unskilled because only the
stupid and unskilled would make such a journey for
little money, troubled the conscience of those who
watched them leave. Women who lived on the moor and
needed the money which the ponies brought, bit their
lips and shook their heads, wishing there were some
other way.

Railways provided another way and in the years
which I remember the ponies were transported by
trucks, their bodies fumbling a kind of pattern as those
which entered first were forced into corners by those
behind. They kept their heads up like breaststroke swim-
mers. When the engine backed against the first truck,
the impact staggered down the line. You could hear the
scrambling, the desperate panting; imagine what would
happen to any head which disappeared. As the engine
slumped forward and the line of trucks crept past us, the
ponies were tilted heads and frightened eyes and the
silence of the crowd was ashamed.

At one time there were about one hundred thousand

ponies working below ground in the coal mines of Britain. We heard rumours of them trapped by run-away tubs; of others working double shifts; of heads crushed and eyes gouged; of bodies scarred by perils which they could not see. In 1887 a Coal Mines Regulation Act had attempted to protect the ponies, but RSPCA inspectors were refused permission to investigate and only miners knew what happened underground. Our town loved the story which filtered from Wales of an old miner who half-killed a youth for ill-treating the fifteen ponies in his care. My mother, who had relatives in Wales, believed the whispers that long confinement in total or semi-darkness made the ponies blind. Others said they became blind only when they came out of the long dark and were dazzled by sunlight.

A Society for the Protection of Pit Ponies was founded in 1927 and tried to fix eleven years as the maximum period for confinement. Its propaganda was strident and determined but could not be effective until changes were effected in the methods of coal production. Mechanization of mines during the 1930s released thousands of ponies, but in 1962 6,471 were still below ground, more than in any other West European country. This number has been gradually reduced and the use of pit ponies will soon cease.

For a while the pony fair seemed to be threatened. Pessimists could see no other use for Dartmoor ponies, almost all of which were mongrels, too small for the shafts of traps or vans although some were used in pony carts. Hill farmers were dismayed by the threatened loss of an easy income. They could not anticipate the post-war demand for riding ponies or the inflation of prices, so that the strong young gelding which you could buy for three pounds before the 1939–45 war became promoted to thirty pounds or more. This meant that a hill farmer with a hundred to sell could anticipate three thousand pounds, almost all of it profit. The highest prices were paid for skewbalds and piebalds, although officially the Dartmoor colours are black, bay and brown, with white vehemently condemned by the Dartmoor Pony Society. But children of the post-war generation liked the 'pretty markings' as children of a previous generation had liked the circus Joey. Parents bought what their children wanted, bidding against each other to inflate prices for types which serious breeders despised.

Hill farmers were not often serious breeders. They produced what the public demanded, turning piebald stallions on to the summer moor in order to ensure parti-coloured offspring. Riding schools and riding stables, expanding to meet week-end and holiday needs, bought small ponies for young riders. Strong Dartmoors were ridden successfully in gymkhanas and hunter trials. The rest were needed for a new trade: the manufacture of pet foods. Because of these developing markets the 1960s were profitable years for the hill farmer who thirty years before might have supposed any demand for mongrel ponies to be virtually over.

The horse fair has also flourished, if in a much more sophisticated form. What used to be an annual fair, important socially as well as commercially, has become a periodic horsemarket which neglects the social trimmings and is concerned only with buying and selling. The organization is efficient. Horses are displayed in pens beneath merciful roofs, exposed to neither sun nor

rain. Potential buyers occupy tiers above a parade ring
like an audience looking down on a sawdust stage. Cata-
logues give the number and details of each animal and
an auctioneer presides with the assistance of a clerk, like
the parson and clerk of nineteenth-century pulpits. One
hundred and twenty horses in a day are not unusual,
although some are sold outside the ring while others do
not reach their reserve.

By the end the auctioneer is hoarse and your feet are
numbed by concrete and the dispersing groups are talking about the highest price, paid for a palomino which
came into the gloom like a memory of sunshine. Horses
of this spectacular colour, golden chestnut with almost
white mane and tail, probably originated amongst the
Barbs and Arabs of the Middle East that were used from
early times to improve Spanish stock and later many
other European horse and pony breeds. Thus palomino-
coloured animals are found both amongst the horses of
the New World, descendants of the Spanish Con-
quistadors' mounts, and in British breeds such as the
Welsh Mountain which have received strong infusions
of Eastern blood from time to time. The palomino has
become very much the Golden Horse of the American
West but does not always breed true to colour. In America it has become established as a breed in itself but
elsewhere still remains defined simply as a colour that
may be seen in an animal of almost any breed.

I try to be rational about the horse market; to tell
myself that it is no less essential and no more squalid
than the weekly trade in cattle. There needs to be a
clearing centre, where those who wish to buy can inspect
a wide variety and unwanted stock can be channelled to

quick slaughter. None can deny that the modern market is much more efficient than the fair; that road transport has quickened and simplified dispersal. But as I listen to myself being rational, I am also listening to a venerable hunter, calling incredulously and looking for someone, sure that this someone doesn't realize he is here and will soon restore him to the place where he belongs. According to the catalogue this hunter carried thirteen stones over rough country for eleven seasons and has neither vice nor blemish. He is offered for sale only 'with regret and to make room for young stock'. More than an old horse is being condemned in that glib phrase.

The truth is I am not one person when I look around a horse market. I am a descendant of the old lady who sat in the dark and worried about coach horses; of the grandmother who worried about Pleasant; of the mother who believed pit ponies to be blind. They are prodding me to do something, because surely I've learned that horses are different. Deprived by man of the security and anonymity which cattle find in a herd, they've become individuals, a fact which Arab tribesmen realized five thousand years ago when they gave their horses names. It's what has happened through five thousand years which makes horses different and shatters the smooth argument about their being just another animal.

For years my family were alarmed that I could be conned by my ancestors into returning from horse markets with the old and the lame and the useless. On one occasion I yielded to family pressure and remained at home while my son and daughter went for the first time and only for a 'look round'. They returned with a borrowed vehicle and a shivering, scrawny thing which seemed to be a filly foal, about nine months old. They said it was five, which a glance at its teeth confirmed. They agreed it was a mongrel runt for which we could have no use at all. Apparently they'd felt 'sorry for it' and had pooled their holiday money to push the price beyond the reach of dealers. They seemed excited by what they had done, unaware or uncaring that they'd been conned by ancestors who could be busy in heads other than mine.

The five-year-old was a cross-bred Dartmoor, about nine hands high; possibly a late foal, doomed in her first year to dead grass and wild weather so that she could not prosper. We gave her the poorest orchard; for a moorland pony, accustomed to living frugally, can be crippled by the rich grass of the valley. She ran into it and for weeks would not come out, apprehensive and miserable, needing a long time to forget whatever had happened since she'd been caught in the 'drift' and put up for sale.

She did not forget until the snow was deep and her grass hidden. Even then she tried to remain independent, digging the snow with a forefoot and finding a little and trying to make it enough. But the snow froze harder and her toes were broken. Finally she was persuaded to come close enough to smell what we were offering. Warm bran smells good to a hungry pony but she was not easily convinced. She made her neck long, watching us as she wondered what would happen if she confessed her dependency and touched whatever it was. She touched and flinched, her nose freckled with the brown stuff. She thought about it and crept another stride, watching us as intently as a cat watching a bird. She touched again and became committed, her eyes still looking up.

It didn't take long after that. She began to follow in our footsteps as though the snow was safe only where we had trod. When we left the gate open she followed us to the back porch and peered to the scullery, exchanging a long stare with the yellow Labrador which wasn't sure what it was supposed to do. No one knows how she first got into the scullery or what curiosity persuaded her up three steps to the door of the farmhouse kitchen. She nudged it open and looked at us. We were eating at the time. It seemed a good idea, so she climbed the last step and passed behind the chairs, peering over our shoulders in the hope of a welcome. That was the day she discovered a taste for cheese.

Soon she became adept at opening doors, because ours are old-fashioned with press-down latches instead of handles. She explored the stone-flagged passage and found the study; startled by the machine-gunning of the typewriter but interested by its margin bell. She came in politely, acknowledging that the dog and cat had their places and must not be disturbed. We got conversational about eleven, when coffee and biscuits were due.

She found other rooms along the passage and reached the lounge which used to be the parlour, nudging the door open and remaining in the doorway until my family complained of the draught. She came in and started, surprised by galloping and gunfire, by images of horses jumping at her. She discovered television with an incredulity which became delight. It's only with difficulty that my sons and daughters restrain her from

Vian Smith and Silver Fiddle, the steeplechaser.

The rosinbacks

The Exmoor

The pair

The author and Juliet, the Dartmoor pony

The barge horse

The cutting horse

Above:
'The Horse of Selene'
from the Parthenon
frieze

Left: The English
thoroughbred

Exercising on the sands

hogging the screen, for she likes to touch as well as observe, trusting nose and nostrils more than eyes. We've
become accustomed to her pattering in for the most
recent instalment of the current Western. It seems long
ago that she was a shivering nonentity, saved by holiday
money from becoming the nothing of a carcass. We call
her Juliet.

9

TIMBER AND STONE

WE knew they'd be coming soon. For days there'd been
the tock of axes on the hill and the terrible sounds of
trees going down. The trees were the beeches which we
had watched change colour with the seasons. They belonged to us because we knew them well and had found
thin, brown nuts beneath them during holidays from
school. They had a name and were a landmark. You
turned left for the sea at Spinners Copse and right if you
were going to the moor.

The town was sad about the trees, half angry that
trees so tall should be cut down for profit. 'In their
prime,' the women mourned, as though the trees were
men, cut down by machine-guns during the first world

war. 'Sixty-footers,' the man guessed, although boys of
the town were sure they were taller. 'As tall as the
church tower,' we insisted, because we could think of
nothing taller.

The hill seemed small, deprived of its individuality,
like a bald head. Great trees did not seem so great when
they were lying down. We couldn't recognize the one
which had given the best nuts. The earth where they had
stood was new and sore, like a battlefield.

The beeches would be taken to the sawmill near the
river where other giants had lain for years, changing
colour during the long process of weathering. Everyone
knew the route they must take, and when the town considered the hazards, its mood changed from mourning
to excitement because our long street was narrow and
had many corners and the question we were asking was,
how could horses get sixty-footers around corners as
sharp as elbows? It had been done before. Old men
boasted they had seen it often. But only by the best
horses. Old men doubted that horses in 1930 could be
good enough.

Four Shire horses were brought from another town.
They were specialists, bred in Lincolnshire which is a
great horse county. They looked enormous in the narrow
street as they passed towards the hill. 'Seventeen hands,'
old men whispered. Each was supposed to be capable of
drawing a load of five tons. 'Net,' the women emphasized, although I wasn't sure what that meant,
having seen it printed on tins of tea and asked questions
which no adult had bothered to answer.

None answered it now for no one had time for anything except the possibility of disaster. They weren't

even interested by what I could tell them about the
Shire; it was descended from the Great Horse of England which had carried knights in heavy armour during
the fifteenth century. I'd read that somewhere and been
surprised, for horses so big must have been slow and I'd
imagined knights galloping to rescue damsels in distress
like the self-appointed heroes of American films. According to this book a knight had needed such a horse
because his weight in full armour had been more than
four hundred pounds and mounting had required pulley
and block as well as moments of comedy and humiliation.

I was as full of these details as a fruit with seed but no
one heeded what I was bursting to confide. They were
following the horses towards the edge of the town; murmuring admiration of the broad strength and rippling
shine of the feathered legs as pale as moonlight. Nervous
traders apologized to customers and put up their shutters, although flimsy wood could not save their windows
if the horses faltered or the long trees swung, aiming tons
like a battering ram. The most nervous trader, pale from
his bake-house heat, ran to the constable, asking if there
was no other way. The constable answered by holding
out his arms, trying to clear the street, to give the team a
chance, although there was plenty of time and the
cranes had not yet lifted the trees to the long, low wagon
which had red mud crusted on its wheels.

We looked up the hill, listening to the shouts, imagining the drama as the first tree rose on iron slings and
swung while voices shouted 'Steady' and the crane
driver chewed the inside of his mouth. The tree swayed
and steadied and inched down, waited a long moment

with daylight still showing beneath, then came down as stealthily as an elephant's foot stepping over a body. Men dragged branches and twigs to the wheels, trying to make a mat which might help. Others secured the first tree with blocks. The foreman beckoned for the next.

The first two trees were of equal girth and length; the third was shorter and rested in the valley formed by the others. Chains went around and were secured by iron hooks. The foreman clambered up to inspect. The driver checked the harness and brought a pair of horses to either side of the long, wooden bar which grew out of the front axle. He remained at their heads while his assistant brought the lead horses and turned them and persuaded them back a stride. The driver fastened the draw chains. Other men retreated, watching him prepare the horses. He was talking to them all the time; conversational talk which seemed right although it would look gibberish in print.

The assistant stood at the head of the near side leader. The driver hung his coat on the hames of his favourite. He glanced towards the path which the horses must take, checking that all litter had been cleared; that nothing remained which could impede the leaders. He nodded to the foreman who signalled to the men. They came to the wheels, their bodies leaning as they braced themselves and waited.

The driver took the whip from around his neck and held it sideways in his right hand. He waited another minute; waiting for silence, absolute silence, so that the horses knew and prepared themselves. He spoke in the special language which they understood. They leaned slightly, tautening the chains. A shine of sweat showed on the youngest horse. The driver let out a long wail and the horses leaned in unison. The wail exploded in a word which all understood. It was 'Now'. Simultaneously the whip cracked.

The horses strained, their great feet chewing the earth. The foreman thought they wouldn't make it. He ran to a wheel, adding his pittance as the men dug their boots. The wheels began to turn. The mat of twigs splintered down. The driver stood back, watching the wheels, watching his team, his voice demanding more, more than the horses seemed able to give. They reached for their dregs and kept giving. The wheels completed the first turn and kept moving, out of the ruts towards firm ground. Men stumbled and straightened, panting a kind of cheer. The driver walked beside his favourite, calling encouragement.

They approached the highway and began a wide, slow arc towards the right; a movement made difficult by the change from earth to tarmac, by the sudden slope which increased the weight. The assistant lowered an iron pan and a wheel rolled into it. The horses crouched their quarters, sitting against the weight. They crept down the slope and the town heard them coming and held its breath, like a nervous city listening to the approach of siege guns. The voice of the driver was the only permitted voice. It was counselling caution, rewarding effort with praise so extravagant that his horses seemed to be heroes.

'So they are,' an old man whispered. 'So they will be if they do it.'

They reached the first houses of the town and windows began to cringe. To occupants looking out it

seemed that something terrible, like death, was passing
and might touch them. When they felt safe, they came
to the street and followed at a distance, relieved that
they were safe, excited by what might happen as the
street narrowed and shop windows became larger. Some
of the shops were lower than the street and this lowness
made the threat bigger and darker. Faces looking up
were round and white. *They'll never do it*. No one put it
into words, but the thought was there, making our
throats tight. We were waiting for the sharpest corner,
called 'Jackson's Corner' because fifty years ago Jackson
had been the town's largest grocer and the windows
which had been his dominated the corner. The horses
prepared for it, each bending a foreleg and keeping the
hoof poised, then putting it down with a quiet sound,
like the clop which a trout makes in the evening river.

The driver came to the head of the near side leader,
looking back to the others and speaking sharply. When
their ears were listening, he began to tell them what he
wanted: *forward now, back me lovelies, steady now*;
inching them to the left while the assistant ran to the end
of the trees, out of sight as he called how many inches,
how close they were to disaster. Faces cringed. You
could hear the fright like waiting for a bomb.

Only the driver did not lose his nerve. He touched the
young horse and called to the others, persuading them
back half a stride and bringing them forward, seeming
to be gaining nothing yet compelling the wheels to make
more space, informed by the unseen voice when he
had won an inch or two. He kept repeating the
manoeuvre, straining our patience so that minutes
seemed long. Tension was shivering in the horses. The

youngest was guttering sweat. The white faced baker
was muttering that he'd known from the first they
wouldn't do it. Then suddenly we realized. The lead
horses were reflected in the watchmaker's window on
the other side of Jackson's Corner. They were getting
round, gaining feet where inches had seemed achievement. Old men glanced to the baker.

The hooves kept moving, slowly up and slowly down,
as though the road were of glass and must not be broken.
The constable hurried towards the roar of a car. It came
towards the crisis, ignorant of what was happening and
made an intruder by ignorance. The uniform waved it
back. There was contempt in the gesture and the town
growled approval, for the street did not belong to
machines today. I remember the car going backwards, like a crestfallen courtier withdrawing from the
throne.

It took nearly an hour to win the battle of Jackson's
Corner and, at the end, the neck of the young horse was
white and all the horses were trembling. The driver
cried congratulations and let them stride two hundred
yards to the steep hill. We filled the street as we followed. I remember grocers' assistants in white aprons
which had frayed edges and reached to their ankles like
backless skirts; carpenters with stubs of flat pencil
pushed beneath their caps; plumbers with tool bags on
their shoulders, held there by hammers inserted in the
rope handles; women with empty baskets; all of them
jubilant, telling each other they might never see the like
again.

The horses reached the steep hill which fell to the
river and was the final test. But it was different now. We

were sure they could do it, could do anything. Their
forelegs stiffened, their hind legs crouched, taking the
pressure on their quarters. The assistant fitted the iron
pans and the driver walked backwards, near the young
horse and watching the others, talking all the time,
making them his handsomes, his beauties, promising it
would be over soon.

It was almost over when they reached the bottom of
the hill. The horses knew it and lengthened their stride,
their feet clopping a rhythm like triumph. Cars in the
square drew back in deference. Modern lorries, considered to be superior to horses, seemed tinpot things by
comparison. Car drivers and lorry drivers, who should
have been the new élite, seemed small compared with
the horseman who had proved himself through his team.
We followed them towards the space beside the river
which was the graveyard of trees.

It was over in one way yet not in another, for the
kitchens and inns of our town would talk about it for ten
years, twenty, forty, and Jackson's Corner would seem a
special place as those who had been there explained how
it had been done, tasting again the alarms and incredulity and jubilation. It's different now. A new road gives
easy access to mills and factories near the river and the
long, narrow street is forbidden to doubledeckers and
coaches and heavy loads. Diesel machines bring timber
to the mill but the town scarcely notices, going about its
business without caring.

The transport of stone has been similarly reduced to a
commonplace. Fifty years ago it was still being done by
barge and barges meant horses and the long creep down
the canal was an adventure in summer, when the fish

T–E

were dozing and the dragonflies were out and village
boys walked beside the barge horse.

The long, shallow barges were linked in groups of
three. Four horses were needed to start them, but as soon
as they were moving and the water was smiling, three
horses were detached and only one continued to plod
the tow path. Slowness was essential, for haste would
have caused waves which would have eroded the banks,
multiplying the costs of maintenance. This insistence on
slowness suited the barge horse, which was often old, its
feet too sore for heavy work on rough roads or cobbles.
Many horses unfit for faster work continued to plod the
tow paths of Britain, drawing loads which would have
needed teams of eight on land.

The first canals were built about 1700, when expanding industries began to demand the fluent and cheap
movement of heavy goods from one town to another or
from mill to port. The traditional means of transport
was still the pack pony and across the Pennines the local
Fell and Dale breeds would continue to be used for about
two hundred years. But even hundreds of ponies on the
pack trails could not meet the need. Wagons were stuck
in winter mud. Steam railways were still a hundred
years away. The immediate answer was water, and by
about 1750 a comprehensive system of inland waterways
was developing. Factories made regular use of them and
the barge horse became among the most important in
the land.

Boys and girls came to the banks to watch the barges
drift as drowsily as punts, their imaginations playing
with ideas about where the barge had come from and
where it was going and what it carried beneath tar-

paulins as secretive as shrouds. There was a comforting quality in the slowness, a sense of inevitability like listening to a long story which you have heard before. Sometimes an old man walked at the horse's head, smoking a clay pipe and dreaming old dreams. Sometimes the horse was ridden by a boy, his legs sticking out uncomfortably on either side. All the horses had names and half the mares seemed to be called Princess or Violet, half the geldings Prince or Brandy. The slowest I ever saw was called Rocket.

The end of the barge horse began with the serious improvement of roads by the combined efforts of two Scots: the gifted amateur John McAdam and the professional engineer Telford. They developed a method of rolling small, graded stones to give a comparatively durable surface, with a system of drains to channel away flood waters. For the first time winter roads were open to transport. The days were almost over when coaches would sink to their axles in mud, when wagons would flounder, compelling drivers either to discard their loads or to seek help from nearby farms.

The transformation was not immediate. There was not enough money. Those who would profit most from good roads were the least able or least willing to pay for them. Estimated costs of maintenance frightened those who were suspicious of change. Tolls were unpopular; toll gates resented. But slowly even remote roads were improved.

This change coincided with the comparatively rapid development of railways, which linked villages with towns and towns with ports, enabling goods to be transported night and day through all the weeks of the year.

By 1900 the barge horse was almost as out-dated as the pack pony, yet it continued to be used in corners of England as the pack pony continued to be used across the Pennines.

The barge horse which I remember best was Violet, a quiet old bay with kind eyes, her feet broken by heavy work on cobbles. She drew three barges containing stone, her plod as reliable as the tick of a clock; not one of those modern clocks which gabble but an old-fashioned clock, which measured time with great care, giving it a special dignity. At the end of her stint Violet stared at you, asking for what she'd been dreaming about during the twelve miles. It was an honour to un-buckle the cheek-piece of her bridle so that the bit fell and left her teeth free; then to raise the nosebag and fasten it around her ears. She ate with a rhythm as steady as the sea.

Ironically the stone which she transported was used for roads which helped to make her canal redundant. It is silent now and the stillness makes it seem deep. There is menace in the stillness and in summer it smells of decay. You can't believe the pride which went into its construction or the purpose which it served when trains were new and toll gates hated. Courting couples strolled beside it. Boys fished and swam and girls picked its tall, wild flowers in bouquets as generous as a wedding. Twice a day they made way for Violet; at ten o'clock passing with her laden barges, at three returning with the empties.

10

HORSES OF FILM AND BOOK

HORSES in the cinema of the 1920s galloped silently. Their sounds came from the piano below the screen, where Mrs MacSomething sat through two performances five evenings a week and three on Saturdays. Her left hand was kept busy during Westerns, pounding the rhythm of the chase as the sheriff's posse followed the bandits towards the hills. By some subtlety of touch she managed to convey a special urgency when the hero's horse appeared; usually white and always the fastest, sometimes travelling alone because the posse was stupid and would be sure to fork left at the trees when all the audience knew the bandits had turned right.

But Westerns were not all guns and galloping. Convention demanded a 'love interest' and although girls thought it 'romantic, just like life', boys dismissed it as 'sloppy stuff'. Some Westerns wasted a lot of time being sloppy; the hero taking off his stetson to show he was a gentleman, the heroine making imploring gestures because it was dangerous out there and he might get killed. We were wiser. We knew that the worst he would get was a flesh wound in the left arm. In our view the heroine was a wearisome burden who tried to come between the hero and heroism.

We knew what was imminent when the piano forgot the heavy stuff and began to trill a 'romantic mood'. Mrs Mac used her right hand for this, tumbling down the high notes in pretty melodies. We expected her to share our boredom, unable to imagine a condition in which romance could seem more important than a six-gun firing twenty-seven times without re-loading; but during one memorable matinee she made her preference plain.

We were barracking a particularly tenacious heroine who insisted on leaning against the door, arms outstretched as she cried, 'No, no,' in goldfish language; so preoccupied with condemning the whole feminine sex, who were plainly superfluous and a burden to men of action, that we didn't realize the trilling had ceased until a shadow darkened us and Mrs Mac was there, as formidable as retribution. She didn't make the mistake for which screen heroines were notorious. She didn't waste time. One clout was enough. Only one of us felt it, but the shock waves passed along the row, compelling us to admit that there might be a point of view other than our own. We made ourselves small, while Mrs Mac returned to the love scene; remaining quiet like so many tortoises in their shells until she called us out with her left hand.

Saturday matinée was our time. Only a few adults were scattered in the ninepenny seats behind us. There were none at all in the seats at the back, which were upholstered pink and cost a shilling and had armrests to keep courting couples apart when the lights were down. The cheapest seats were in front, within a few strides of the screen. They were the sixpennies for evening performances and no girl over fourteen would be 'seen dead in them', since occupation of the sixpennies denoted poverty and those girls who had to pay for themselves out of the meagre wage which fourteen-year-olds received when they left school, saved for two weeks so that they could display themselves in the ninepennies and keep their self-respect.

On Saturday afternoons the sixpennies became the threepennies, which still seemed expensive to those who had watched Fatty Arbuckle for a penny before the 1914–18 war. We earned our threepences in various ways: as errand boys and milk-round boys, by holding horses on market days. The smartest among us traded in horse manure, shovelled from the cobbles when market day was over and barrowed to an old gentleman who was eccentric enough to be courteous to children and generous enough to pay a penny a load.

Apparently he loved his garden and believed horse manure to be ideal for roses. In the interest of trade we took a proprietary interest, comparing his blooms with those grown by the pig muck fanatic down the road and assuring him that he had twice as many. The old gentleman was glad to hear it, but the neighbour had revenge by winning the battle of the tomatoes; for which reason I have gone through life advocating horse manure for roses and pig muck for tomatoes, heedless of those expert gardeners who claim to know better.

The programme began with a two-reeler, often made by Hal Roach and sometimes featuring sorrowful Laurel and bullying Hardy or Harry Langdon or Patsy Kelly and Thelma Todd. It was followed by the serial which had twelve episodes, each ending in a crisis which the following week proved to be much less perilous than we had hoped. Tom Mix, who rode a horse called Tony, was fading out as the Saturday hero; Buck Jones, whose white stallion responded to a whistle, was still heroically on the side of law and order in the fashion established by G. N. Anderson, who was the first 'Western hero' and became famous as Bronco Billy.

Often the main feature was another Western, different from the serial only because it had more horses and bigger fights and more spectacular feats of heroism. Our Saturday entertainment used dozens of horses, sometimes hundreds, and this was not surprising since from the first the camera had been fascinated by the horse.

Early 'movies' tried to catch the fluent movement, the wonderful marriage of power and grace. One did more than follow the movement in detail; it settled the old controversy about whether a horse at any time takes all feet from the ground during the rhythm of the gallop. Edward Muybridge, an Englishman in California, provided proof in 1872. His series of photographs showed that a horse is for a split second suspended in mid air during the gallop; seeming to be flying as the myth-makers believed when they invented Pegasus and gave him wings. From that year the work of minor artists became outdated. Their work showed horses galloping with forelegs stretched forward and hind legs stretched backward in a sprawl as implausible as it was ugly.

Another early 'movie' showed horses trotting. The movement was jerky, as far from life as a marionette, but any movement was a minor miracle and crowds paid to see a crude representation of what they could see for nothing a hundred times a day. One hero of an early newsreel was Persimmon, which won the Derby in 1896. The colt was owned by the Prince of Wales, son of Queen Victoria and soon to become King Edward VII. London audiences rushed to see a film of Persimmon winning by a neck from St Frusquin.

In 1903 came the first film to tell a story. It was 'The Great Train Robbery', directed by Andrew Porter who could not have known what he was starting when he directed actors to hold up a mail train, then to attempt escape on horseback. The law gave chase, also by horse, and the final sequence became a convention of the Western.

By the 1920s, when we sat wide-eyed in the three-pennies, it was understood that crime does not pay, that the pursuers must somehow out-ride the law breakers to enforce justice in the final reel. At the same time we were invited to associate white with heroism and black with villainy, although no one told us that by using these elementary symbols films were continuing an ancient tradition. Medieval art depicted saints and heroes riding white horses; while Satan, as the Prince of Darkness, was given a black stallion because black was night and night was fear. Christian legends of Europe were similar to the pagan of North America, where Indian tribes heard galloping in thunder and invented an evil horse which galloped down the sky, striking lightning from its hooves.

But we weren't concerned about the ancient origin of Hollywood symbolism. We knew what side to be on as soon as we saw the horses. White was 'ours' and certain to win. Black was the 'away team', which would seem to be winning only until the final reel. This certainty was comforting and the film-makers of the 1920s knew better than to confuse us by having good and evil change horses.

Early Westerns owed part of their popularity to this predictability. Another essential was a bloodless form of violence, which demanded that men should fall dead without seeming to be hurt. But clever directors began to tinker with the formula. More than men had to fall. Horses had to fall also and the more spectacular sequences showed horses brought down in full gallop, apparently within inches of the camera. We were asked to gasp in surprise, to applaud the technical ingenuity and to admire the dramatic inventiveness. But at the back of our minds we began to wonder. Did the fallen get up? Could they get up? Were they broken by trip wires? And if so, could such calculated and rehearsed cruelty be justified artistically or commercially?

I wasn't worried about famous horses – including Trigger, the palomino stallion owned by Roy Rogers, which was so precious that it had its own contract with Republic Pictures. Those which worried me were the nonentities, as easily replaced as faces in a crowd. My delight in the Western faded as I became old enough to ask questions which no one wanted to answer. I could not undertand why crude spectacle was considered to be commercially more viable than veracity; why a director did not show a cowboy and his horse cutting a calf from a herd, working together with harmony and lightning reflexes. It seemed to me that to incorporate such a genuine spectacle of horsemanship within the 'Western' formula would be more relevant than Trigger shamming dead, and would contribute more to the American legend than horses falling on tripwires in celebration of battles.

The small screen of television has taken the place of the Saturday matinée, but the Western persists, as popular with the young as it was to us in the threepennies. The crudities persist also. I'm still offended by the yanking around of horses which seem bewildered or humiliated; still worried by horses which are brought down in the hope of surprising or thrilling somebody. Commercial exploiters of the American myth continue to show little respect for the animal which drew wagons, logged timber, herded cattle; which was for a hundred years man's only means of creating new prosperity out of old wilderness.

The modern cinema, technically superb, much more sophisticated than that of thirty years ago, uses horses vulgarly in pseudo-Biblical and fake historical extravaganzas. Few directors attempt to catch the poetic simplicity which Denys Colomb de Daunant touched in his classic *A Dream of Wild Horses*. This shows white horses of the Carmargue splashing in the sea. Its slow motion exposes their marvellous grace, and because beauty is always new, this film will remain new no matter how often we see it. One of the few British films in which horses were used poetically was *Henry V*, which set a new standard of perception as the chargers of Agincourt moved towards each other.

Horses tend to be more enduring in print because good books tend to be re-issued more frequently than good films. Probably the most famous horse of any medium is Black Beauty; a Victorian carriage horse, almost ruined by broken knees and the fashionable bearing rein, finally rescued by grandfather Thoroughgood and grandson Willie, then restored to dignity by kind Joe and three ladies. This sentimental life story, written in the first person without apology, has been read by every generation since 1887. It has been translated into German, Italian and French and continues to be read by the young, although its reforming purpose was long ago exhausted.

Anna Sewell wrote it in middle age and got it published when she was fifty-seven. It was her only book. Lame from childhood and isolated by her infirmity, she was the daughter of a bank manager at Brighton, to which town the upper middle-class repaired in summer, when convention demanded an exodus from London. She had ample opportunity to observe the petty tyrannies which they inflicted on their carriage horses. The most persistent was the 'bearing rein', a device to hold a horse's head high in a travesty of being smart or 'showy'. Such restraint placed continual strain on the muscles of the neck and distorted the windpipe, making breathing difficult, finally causing the condition known as 'roaring'. On a hill a horse could not lower its head for serious pulling and was whipped for being slow or lazy. When going down the other side it could not see the road, stumbling so often that scarred knees were the badge of the former carriage horse in its old age.

By the mid-Victorian years, fashion had thought of something else; a bearing rein which was also a gag, equipped with a hoop on the curb bit to keep the tongue from lolling. The bar of the curb passed beneath the tongue to press on the most sensitive part of the mouth – a refinement which ensured immediate response to even the least persuasive hands. It was considered smart to have your horses foaming from the corners of their mouths and if the foam was stained red it could be considered proof that they were 'mettlesome' and 'on their toes'.

Professional coachmen yielded to the demands of employers who, knowing nothing about horses, insisted on a

turn-out which exactly resembled those of their social rivals. Carters followed the fashion, so that even dray horses, hauling heavy loads, were unable to lower their heads during long pulls. This fashion astonished Germany, where coachmen kept their horses with heads permanently tied down; while both English and German fashions caused derision in France and Russia, where horses' heads were always free. Travellers reported that horses in the streets of Moscow were wild and difficult to control; a fable welcomed by those in London who had a commercial interest in the design and sale of new equipment.

Saddlers kept introducing new devices because each innovation was good for trade, while dealers advocated the bearing rein at all costs, especially the gag type because it broke mouths as well as spirit and ensured a continual demand for new horses. Members of the RSPCA were among the guilty. They were said to drive to humanitarian meetings behind horses tightly reined and gagged.

It was against this background that the semi-invalid wrote her protest which was also a love story. She died the year after *Black Beauty* was published, unaware that its distribution would coincide with the development of compulsory education. For the first time children of working-class parents could read. They read *Black Beauty* and wept. As propaganda against the bearing rein in particular and against fashionable barbarities in general, it was more effective than polite appeals by the RSPCA to 'Please give the horse his head when going uphill'.

By the middle of the twentieth century, the horse, as

the hero of fiction, was no novelty. *My Friend Flicka* was a best-seller in the USA, although the commercial success of *National Velvet* derived less from the horse which competed in the Grand National than from the social caricatures. The American story has dignity and charm; the English has neither because farce can have neither. A film was made of *National Velvet*, with Elizabeth Taylor and Mickey Rooney being young, and Donald Crisp being sturdy. Its version of the Grand National is hilarious or ludicrous, depending on your point of view.

Of much less renown and much greater quality is *Smoky*, an American story told with authority and zest. It touches your heart and keeps touching although you've read the whole several times and know that at the end the cow pony turned rodeo horse, which hated Mexicans and was humiliated by work between shafts, will be restored to the old man at the ranch. It's another love story and it's the love which cannot be faked.

I began to write about horses when I was eight, illustrating the stories with sketches, unaware that this need to portray and at the same time to pay tribute was as old as the prehistoric sketches on the walls of caves in southern France and Spain. All my horses had two legs, because I wasn't sure what they did with those on the other side. Despite this handicap they never walked. They were always galloping. Like the horses of Westerns, they never paused to eat or sleep; both of which I considered, at eight, to be a waste of time.

The following year my mother provided an old typewriter and a hassock to make the chair high enough. From that birthday I was always writing. The stories

were as private as a diary. I don't know what happened
to them and had forgotten them until a few years ago,
when I discovered exercise books filled with stories about
wonderful horses. They could have been written by me
at the age of nine. In fact they were the work of my sons
and daughters, who had also felt the need to portray and
exalt. It shows how one generation resembles another
without being aware.

In 1961 I wrote *Question Mark*, which was about a
horse of doubtful pedigree; and the success of this novel,
especially in America (where it had another title) encouraged more, each needing at least one horse, not
necessarily successful or elegant but towering above
others in its individuality. King Sam was one. Others
were Dunfermline and Pilgrim Star and The Lord
Mayor.

All are alive in various parts of the world, surviving
translation as they stride into the imaginations of young
readers. The wonderful quality about horses of your invention is that they do not grow old or deteriorate. They
are preserved as you wanted them to be at the time of
creation. You have only to open *The Horse of Petrock* to
find Dunfermline still running although the horse from
which she was painted is long dead; only to read *Come
Down the Mountain* to find Pilgrim Star still recovering
from neglect although the attempt in life was not wholly
successful and the original had to be destroyed. The most
recent invention is The Minstrel Boy, a big, dark brown
horse which dominates an adult novel published in
Britain and the U.S.A.

All are re-creations of the real and all are different
because no horse exactly duplicates another. It's the

differences which express the individuality and it's the individuality which fascinates. If Question Mark remains a favourite it is only because he was the first. It's no coincidence that in 1970 the family racing colours have a yellow question mark on the front and back of the red jersey.

II

THE RACES

MY first racehorse was a small bay with big knees and
sad eyes, and what I remembered best are his ears. They
were long and limp and because they drooped when he
was pensive, race day crowds thought he was stupid. I
wish he could have confounded derision by winning in a
canter, telling the mockers to take it out of that; but in
the years of our acquaintance he never won anything
and seemed not to think he could.

He was mine for three days a year when he came to
our town for the September meeting and was stabled at
the London Inn, where stage coaches had pulled in a
hundred years before. There were stables on the race
course but not enough to accommodate all the horses

which would run in twelve races. Those which could not be accommodated there were sent to stables in the town; some of which were supposed to be dark slums. But the London Inn was proud of its stables and of the coaching history which they represented. A week before the meeting, when the landlord knew how many horses were coming, the litter which had accumulated during the year was broomed out and walls were whitewashed, troughs scrubbed, doors made new with creosote.

Provision of straw for bedding was the landlord's responsibility and he made that responsibility a pride. It was always wheat straw, less edible and more absorbent than that of oat or barley. One of the old men who lived in a corner of the bar, never seeming to eat as though he needed only pipe and pint, was employed by the landlord to prepare each bed with out-dated skill.

He placed the straw in a criss-cross pattern so that urine would leak through and leave the top straw clean. In those days, when corn was harvested by reaper and handled with respect, wheat straw was never less than nine inches long and one of the incidental skills of the stableman was this criss-cross pattern done with such swift economy that it seemed easy. The straw was thickest around the walls, forming high cushions to protect legs, and back when the horse lay down or to prevent him becoming cast if he rolled.

A horse can rise only by straightening his forelegs. If he rolls so near a wall that his forelegs cannot straighten, he is a semi-prisoner and will struggle, wrenching muscles and inflicting internal injuries which might be difficult to treat or even to diagnose. A horse is most likely to become *cast* when he is in a strange stable, and might struggle for hours before the top door opens and somebody looks in. By then he is exhausted and unable to race for days.

My favourite old man, whose pipe trembled between his gums, told me this in a mumble as he billowed the straw. He liked to talk as he worked and it was through him that I heard about the old days, when horses walked from meeting to meeting, ignoring the railways as dangerous and expensive. Steady exercise was good for their feet and legs, healthier or at any rate cheaper than confinement in a truck. They walked from twenty to thirty miles a day, sometimes grazing at nights near the road while their lads improvised beds out of coats and slept like cowboys, each with a saddle for his pillow.

I wondered what had happened when it rained, but you weren't supposed to ask questions. You were supposed to believe that such Spartan travel had kept horses tough, their legs slicked by dew, their feet kept hard by walking; making them less prone to injuries than the pampered thoroughbreds of modern times and much less afflicted by boredom.

The old man believed boredom to be as harmful to the horse as it is to man; that it encourages mischief of the mind, expressed by horses in crib-biting and wind-sucking, by tail-rubbing and a restless weaving. He thought horses should come hungry to their trough and tired to their bed.

His prejudice over-simplified the problems of keeping horses fit, but there was good sense behind it. Walking never hurt a horse while short periods of grazing stimulate its appetite for dry or artificial foods. Boredom is a burden to an animal confined for about twenty-two hours a day and as many injuries are inflicted during these periods of boredom as during the hours of work. He was right to insist that the racehorse of the nineteenth century was tougher than its modern counterpart, capable of running twice in an afternoon and winning twice; but what he omitted to stress was the change in standards. Small races of the nineteenth century were slow, capable of being won by part-breds and by hunters which would be considered out-classed a hundred years later.

Two hours before the horses arrived the stables were new and exciting; the walls as white as surplices, emphasizing the yellowness of straw and darkness of creosote. The creosote was not only a gesture towards proper maintenance. It gave the wood a bitter taste, sufficient to discourage all save the most perverse from random gnawing. If you kept quiet and believed everything the old man said, you were allowed to broom the yard, where coaches had stood while ostlers had changed teams. Windows of the inn still looked down like theatre boxes to a stage and faces were still at the lattice, speculating about what horses would come and if they would win, arguing about the great year when horses from the London Inn had won eight races in two days, showering riches on the customers, none of whom dared admit he'd backed something else.

The horses came by train. Boys of the town were at the station to watch it steam in and shrug off the boxes. A shunting engine, nicknamed Puffing Billy, shunted the boxes to a siding where hatch doors opened and the lads appeared.

They were always lads in stable jargon, although some were grey and wizened. Others were semi-gypsies,

wild of hair and dark of tan; what my mother called
'race day roughs' who slept beside their horses either in
drunken stupor or because their employers, called their
masters by racing authorities, refused to pay two
shillings a night for a bed. Some were Irish. Some were
orphanage lads, compelled at fourteen to find a substitute for home in licensed stables, where discipline was
cruder than in the Services but made tolerable by the
prospect of sudden reward. The lad who 'did' a good
horse could expect gifts from a grateful owner. If he was
denied a good horse and had to make do with screws and
nags and scrubbers, there was always the hope of picking
up 'whispers' like a radio sensitive to unseen voices. If
the 'whispers' were right, he could turn shillings into
pounds; making more in ten minutes than a skilled
craftsman earned in a month. This seemed madness to
my mother and to those craftsmen who backed losers.

Elder lads, those with grey hair and an ingrained contempt of the young, were as elegant as the grooms of
private stables; their boots and leggings polished to a
brown shine, their shirt sleeves rolled meticulously to
their elbows. They were expert in the rolling of sleeves;
for some reason despising sleeves cut short, using their
tight and tidy rolling to reproach young lads who were
sloppy and without pride.

Two horses for the Lord Nelson Inn were unloaded.
We watched the lad pass out sacks of oats and trusses of
hay, the hamper which contained paddock sheets and
night rugs and brushes. A railway uniform, helping in
the hope of picking up a 'whisper', which would prove
more valuable than a formal tip, transferred the miscellany to the cart of the town porter; stacking it in a

corner to ensure sufficient space for the sacks and hampers which would be taken to other inns.

There were stories of the town porter confusing the consignments, delivering hay at the London which should have gone to the Waterman's, thereby provoking jealous fighting among the lads and prejudicing the outcome of races. I began to understand that it was not enough to have hay. It had to be the type to which a horse had become accustomed. A sudden change could worry a potential winner. One trainer, making water as important as hay, insisted that his horses were accompanied by churns, filled at their home pump. A horse drinks about eight gallons a day, so each of his horses needed two twelve gallon churns to cover the period of the meeting. Three or four horses could mean as many as eight churns, which made railway uniforms groan and the town porter mutinous.

The town porter wore a peaked cap and smelled of snuff. His horse was a grey which had turned white in old age. It moved away as the racehorses appeared, like the humble moving from royalty. Boys of the town habitually derided its dipped back and tragic bones, but on the eve of a race meeting, when its poverty was emphasized by the shine of thoroughbreds, the joke became sour. We felt sorry for it as it plodded towards the town, distributing better food than ever it had tasted.

Some horses wore leather pads to protect their knees. Others had rubber pads between their ears, protecting sensitive polls from random blows when trucks were being shunted. Railway staffs were supposed to take special care of horses during transit, but we'd seen what happened to calves in hessian and chicks in boxes, to homing pigeons in hampers. We thought trainers were right to take elaborate precautions.

The horses came down the ramps with more curiosity than apprehension. Some were hurdlers, with small heads and sharp ears. A few were steeplechasers, their withers high and their legs long, their travelling bandages hiding the scars of firing. Experienced lads handled them casually, always on a long leading rein. You could tell the inexperienced by his need to grasp the rein near the head-collar.

Sometimes professionals needed help. A lad with three horses could not lead them simultaneously. He needed help from town boys, giving them the honour of leading the probable winner of the second race on Wednesday or the veteran which had fallen in the Grand National of 1931 and would run in the three-mile steeplechase on Thursday. He walked in front, looking back to the volunteers, shouting to the 'townie' who was leading on the off side and with his left hand, rebuking him because it confused the horse which was accustomed to being led on the near side and by the right hand. Sometimes he called back questions, asking which way to the Waterman's. There were few cars or motor vans in the early 1930s and they immediately conceded right of way. The greatest hazard was the blue bus which once an hour came to the square. It was the only vehicle which felt important enough to challenge the ancient right of horses.

I waited for those destined for the London Inn. Three came out with heads high and feet lilting, their bandaged tails extended in what seemed to be banners of pride. The fourth to appear was small and dull and perpetually preoccupied, sliding down the ramp and waiting for something to happen like a browned-off soldier who has travelled too often. This was mine. I approached him with what amounted to a handshake, making it a kind of reunion which at least one of us appreciated. Railway uniforms called him Old Loppy because of his ears and it is by this name that I remember him; although racecards pretended he was Prince Something, a remote descendant of The Tetrarch and St. Simon, with others in his pedigree which were to racing what the Cecils were to the House of Lords.

A junior lad, with black hair and gypsy eyes and Killarney in his voice, took the first horse. The senior lad, who wore a yellow waistcoat and brown breeches, with a tweed cap to deny his baldness, followed with two others. I was in the middle with the dunce. We proceeded in triumph from the railway to the town, bringing people from shops and kitchens, men from ladders as they asked the names of the horses and if their time had come for winning.

There was a strong belief among workmen that while racing was 'The Sport of Kings', it was also corrupt. Minor hurdle races and steeplechases were believed to be so 'fixed' that almost every horse achieved victory during the season; by which amiable arrangement small trainers were able to stay in business while the owner of a mediocre horse could make a profit by backing it only when success was guaranteed.

This arrangement could never have been as amiable or infallible as the credulous supposed, but belief that it existed invested accident or error with sinister undertones. If the favourite fell at the last fence, it was not an accident and the jockey was only feigning injury. It was part of an elaborate plot to allow the 20–1 outsider to win. Or if a horse ran out at a fence or swerved through a wing or passed the wrong side of a marking flag or was brought down by other fallers; if it refused at the open ditch or was pulled up without obvious signs of injury, clever faces in the crowd immediately smelled corruption and for weeks afterwards men in overalls described how it had been done and why, mourning less the corruption than the secrecy which had excluded them.

But on the day before a meeting there was no suspicion; only a rising excitement, sharpened by the prospects of sheaves of fivers which would prove that racing was honest after all. There were even those who asked about Loppy. Would he win tomorrow? If the question was aimed at me, my response was always a smiling silence; implying a trickery too deep to be casually revealed. What wounded me most was for Loppy to be ignored. On these occasions I whispered to him to do something, somehow to prove himself; imagining the consternation if he won by twenty lengths from the astonished favourite. Every year the dream seemed plausible during the long walk to the London Inn.

Loppy had the box in a corner, where the sun never reached. He walked in without surprise or protest, lowering his head to breathe questions over the straw, then looking around for hay and water. When he was sure about them he chose his place and stared at me in concentration, his body stiffening as he widened his hind legs and passed urine. By this act he put his smell into the box and made it his. He always did it within minutes, but the senior lad told me of horses which fretted for hours, unable to pass their mark. There were even those which could never do it in a strange box. Their racing had to be restricted to meetings which they could reach within hours.

Old Loppy always stood and dreamed while I brushed him, awakening only when the brush passed between his front legs which was his ticklish place. He seemed to be remarkably sensible, but the conduct of others persuaded me that this was not how a fit race-horse should behave. The horse next door was writhing and snapping, earning the reproaches and simultaneously the respect of the Irish lad. It began to lurch its back legs, kicking the partition in thuds which rose and kept rising until they were higher than my head. This was supposed to be the exuberance of a potential winner, but I cringed and thanked heaven for Loppy.

Faces came from the windows to inspect. It was important that horses stabled at the London Inn should

win more races than those stabled at the Lord Nelson
and Waterman's Arms and Saracen's Head. Prestige as
well as silver was at stake. The faces asked questions but
the lads confided little; only that the horses had been
'brought up from grass' in the middle of July and were in
their sixth week of work. I gathered they were not yet
fully fit and had come to our meeting only to get 'wound
up' for more valuable races in the autumn. But the faces
didn't believe it. They remembered last year when
horses recently 'brought up' had won four races in two
days.

The lads worked quickly, with their coats off and
sleeves rolled; hissing between their teeth, fretting their
brushes against curry combs and tapping white dust
from the crevices. They were always hurrying. Their
footsteps gabbled as they brought buckets and hay,
tipped corn into troughs for the largest meal of the day.
By six o'clock top doors were closed and bolted, osten-
tatiously padlocked by the senior lad who retained the
keys. Loppy was given the broken lock, which would
open if you tapped it.

The lads departed to wash at the pump and to change
their shirts, emerging spick-and-span in the bar where
the landlord had drinks drawn in readiness. I was free to
wander the yard, guarding Loppy from the crime which
I'd read about. Nat Gould was the racing novelist of
those days. He wrote about doping and crime rings, and
my evening was given to frightening myself with im-
aginary perils. Usually I had to be sent home by the
landlord.

It was a long night, spent waiting for dawn and the
excuse to be up and running to the yard where Loppy's

top door was the last to open. He came to the half door and blew his nostrils and waited politely, betraying no jealousy when two of the other horses were saddled and ridden to the field called Sanctuary. They were cantered briefly in what the senior lad called a 'pipe-opener'. When they came back, they were accompanied by a dapper little man who wore his soft hat at a perky angle. He was the trainer. I gathered he had arrived the previous evening and had booked at the town's largest hotel. He watched the horses being watered for the last time and given a light breakfast of bruised oats. They would not drink or eat again until their races were over.

The windows of the inn watched the trainer closely, trying to read his manner, to guess if he was pleased. At eleven o'clock the owners appeared with their wives and daughters. There were small conferences in corners of the yard and the windows strained to hear. But Loppy's owner never came. The horse was made conspicuous by neglect, like the hospital patient who receives no visitors.

The windows deduced what they could from the arrival of the farrier; one of the four blacksmiths who shod the town's vanners and carthorses. He removed iron shoes and substituted steel plates; each weighing five ounces, twice as heavy as aluminium yet much lighter than iron. The horses knew what the plating signalled. They sidled and kicked, stinging the farrier's face with their tails. It was the landlord's task to keep strangers from the yard, to pretend not to know which were being plated. They never plated Loppy. He ran all his races with iron shoes, worn as thin as sixpences.

Twelve o'clock on race day was a special time. You

could feel the hurry as building workers took off overalls, as women hurried from shops and girls from factories and clerks from offices. Some shops were preparing to close, making an afternoon of sport more important than the possibility of selling shoes or kettles, but those owned by Methodists and Congregationalists and Wesleyians and Plymouth Brethren never did, because racing was gambling and gambling was a sin. Moreover, hundreds were coming from the rural district and each was a potential customer. The Plymouth Brother who was also the barber was always busy on race days, for rural workers would not go to the races until their hair was cut and smelling of brilliantine.

My father hurried with a long stride. If he backed winners this afternoon, he would attend again to-morrow. Otherwise the first half-day of the meeting was his only holiday of the year apart from Bank Holidays. He was a prudent man and hated racing because he hated losing; but he also loved it because he loved winning and the excitement in his face when he won four and ninepence made it plain to me that this was special money, subtly different from four and nine earned by his tools. He was a carpenter and a good one. He wanted me to be the same and wouldn't listen when I wanted to be a jockey.

I wanted this most on race days. The rest of the year I was prepared to settle for groom or coachman or van driver. I didn't much care as long as it guaranteed work with horses, but my father kept sawing and planing, refusing to listen to anything except a trade. If he knew about Loppy and my part in race days, he gave no sign.

My part became public an hour before the race, when I was given the greatest honour of my year. The senior lad brushed Loppy and blanketed him and painted his feet with oil. He clipped a leading tape to the off side bit-ring, passed it through the nearside and gave it to me making Loppy mine for perhaps fifteen minutes. We passed solemnly down the street towards the racecourse, me talking to him without saying a word, Loppy answering with his ears; a communion of silence which sometimes brought our heads together like the back row of the cinema on Saturday nights.

He showed no fear of traffic, retiring politely to the gutter as the blue bus approached. Even the funfair, which occupied the acre where the small circus had been, did not interest him. He passed it without a glance, seeming to be preoccupied by something very deep. Through the trees I could see the bobbing caps which said that a race was being run. There were red and white flags, white rails, birch fence as neatly trimmed as sub-urban hedges; but Loppy had seen too many race-courses. He went towards racing like an absent-minded professor towards a classroom.

We followed other horses to the gate. You needed no official pass in those days; no passport photograph or signature or proof of identity. To be leading a horse was enough. Gates opened all the way to the paddock and this was my reward; for I could not have bought a place among the bowler hats and tweeds and shooting-sticks.

The junior lad took over, flashing complaint because I was late. I watched the trainer sponge Loppy's eyes and nostrils; place number cloth and weight cloth; tighten the girths of the lightweight saddle and pass a surcingle over it. The jockey was an Irish boy called O'Something, a novice soon to become famous. When he needed to lose weight, he slept in a manure heap, using its heat to sweat off pounds as more sophisticated professionals used the Turkish bath. Presumably one of the purposes which Loppy served was giving experience to promising apprentices.

Five minutes before the advertised time of the race he was walking around the ring, still solemn and pre-occupied, content to be last of eight even during the preliminaries.

The racecourse was a former wilderness near the river. It was shaped like an O which has been sat on and the stretch near the river seemed far away and empty, occu-pied only by ambulance uniforms and by families who picnicked between races, the mothers knitting while their children ran imitation races. Bookmakers were near the stand and crowds approached them with hands lifted, like sinners at a revivalist meeting pleading for salvation. I watched them exchange silver for tickets and place the tickets carefully in their pockets and caps. Their hurry was nervous. They'd been warned about pickpockets and bag-snatchers. They'd read about razor gangs. Their faces seemed different from those in a street; for faces in a street have many thoughts while these had only one.

The stand which seemed so august was only a series of wooden tiers, its roof supported by wooden pillars which obscured your view. I envied the bowler hats their places of privilege and found another near the rail, leaning to see the horses come to the track. They seemed many for eight was a large field. Loppy was fourth as they walked by, chewing his bit and looking down like one who has lost something but cannot remember where. When they turned at the end of the parade, he did not throw up his head or plunge or pretend enthusiasm. His response was mechanical. He cantered past with his ears flopping and I called to him without speaking, begging him to show them.

It was a race of two miles and eight hurdles. The hurdles were three feet six inches high, made of gorse on wooden frames which leaned; ready to be knocked down by forelegs or dragged down by hind legs. The jockeys' colours made a ragged line and waited for the starter's flag. The sound from the stand, a wordless mumble like the grumble of the sea, told you that the flag had fallen, that the colours were advancing although you couldn't see or hear. Seconds passed before you heard the drumming and the breathing, the clatter of hooves on wood as they jumped the first. They came into view on your right and suddenly you didn't want to see. Loppy had ceased to be a ten-year-old gelding with big knees. He'd become a red cap and the red cap was in the middle of the tumult. I imagined him bumped by horses on either side, struck into by horses behind. For the first time I realized how he hated it.

They turned towards the river and took their sounds with them, compelling you to wait and wonder, to suffer in your imagination and at the same time to hope, because it might be different today. It never was. Once Loppy fell in the silence near the river, reappearing without his jockey and looking for the paddock as though for a welcome. Usually he found gaps in the hurdles and survived, returning only thirty seconds late to an ironic cheer. The jockey slid down with a growl of disgust and dragged off the saddle, abandoning him to the junior lad who smeared his sweat with warm water, half doing it because there was another horse in the next race and this horse was more important because it might win.

I was allowed to take over; holding Loppy with one hand and lifting the browband of the bridle to squeeze water around his ears. The bottoms of his ears were always sore because they were large and the bridle was small. He lifted his head and nudged me to hurry, his eyes narrowed and trembling from the dribbles. He raised a back foot to show me where another itch was and I crouched to reach the tender stifle within the back leg, smearing the sweat and squeezing a white scum into the bucket, surprised by how much even an abject failure had to give during a hurdle race.

The trainer came to watch me draw the scraper down the dark shine. He didn't speak. He seemed accustomed to anonymous boys. He emptied the bucket and half-filled it at the tap, inviting Loppy to drink and slapping his neck with a disdain which seemed cheerful and affectionate. Loppy drank deeply. You could see it going down his throat. He slobbered over the pool at the bottom but the trainer would not give him more; not until he was dry and returned to the London Inn.

At five o'clock, when the last race was being run, we left the racecourse and climbed the long, steep street; towards an inn which was jubilant because both the plated horses had won. The senior lad brought damp bran and Loppy ate it solemnly while the winners fretted, unable to eat, spilling bran from the corners of their mouths, their eyes still wild with the strain of endeavour. I remember wondering about this sport which made people rich and horses old. I'd heard it called the 'Sport of Kings' but it seemed also to be the sport of craftsmen and labourers and swindlers; of hard men who did not care about the horses.

On Friday morning it was over. Horses were led to the railway station and temporary stables were abandoned. At the London Inn, black hens moved in to scavenge the straw and to lay in Loppy's trough. Casual labourers, drafted from the Labour Exchange at ninepence an hour, were sweeping the litter of betting tickets and cartons, those thin green packets which used to hold five cigarettes when five cigarettes cost twopence. They pored over the mess like beachcombers, seeking small silver and coppers, keys and rings for which owners might give rewards. Meanwhile the town went back to work, counting the cost in work at one shilling and threepence an hour; rueful yet not repentant, aware that despite laments about fallen favourites and crooked jockeys, they would respond again next year when the local newspaper announced record entries.

There is no race-meeting at our town now. The fixture was abandoned during the 1939-45 war, considered superfluous to a sport which was becoming increasingly sophisticated and would soon be a popular spectacle on television. What was the racecourse is now put to less spectacular, less social and much more practical uses; but memories are there and Loppy is among them, for ever panting in pursuit like the brave but backward pupil who knows he will never catch up.

12

SUNDAY MORNING

SUNDAY morning is the time for leaning on doors to talk about horses; good horses and bad, eccentrics which walk all night and will not lie down, wilful old characters which are sly and clever, wonderful horses which never realized their potential because of accident or stupidity or something undefinable called luck.

You need luck with horses which is why horsemen are superstitious; not least when they plait a mane in seven knots because seven is a lucky number or nail a horseshoe above a door. The shoe should be upward to form a cup. Nail it askew and your luck spills. Nail it upside down and your luck runs out. Superstition is fortified by sentiment when the shoe is from a favourite horse; best of all an aluminium racing plate, removed from a winner with the cheers still in the clouds.

Sunday is traditionally a relaxed day, although it might be the busiest where horses are at livery or are available for hire. Only the essentials get done and there is time for dreaming. Men have been dreaming about the perfect horse for hundreds of years but it wasn't until the seventeenth century that they began to get the dream into focus; visualizing an animal so refined that all blemishes would be bred out and all virtues exalted. Strength, speed and courage were the primary virtues; although there was a fourth, less easy to define or talk about, essentially that elegance which the Greeks tried to catch when they carved cavalcades in stone. Tribes of Arabia had a word for what these men were striving for. It was 'Kehilan', meaning *thoroughbred*.

It was no fluke that the foundation stallions of the English thoroughbred came from the Middle East. The Barb, the Arab and the Turk had become renowned for their speed and toughness. The Byerley Turk was imported into England in 1689. He represented a breed which had speed and courage yet was seldom considered elegant. The Darley Arabian and Godolphin Arabian represented a breed which was not only the oldest and by eighteenth-century standards the fastest, but was also the most beautiful. Humble men became artists in their heads when they regarded the best of the Arab breed. They sighed for the power to catch and somehow to preserve the wonderful beauty of stillness as well as the grace of movement.

These stallions were mated with native mares or with mares also introduced from the Middle East. Their early progeny were not tall by modern standards; fourteen-three hands was average. Neither were they fast by comparison with the modern racehorse. But their feats were enough to excite the imaginations of the wealthy, who invested private fortunes in improving the standard so that within a hundred years four inches were added to the average height and half minutes clipped off racing times.

Times were not recorded for the Derby from its inception in 1781 to 1845; but the time officially recorded by the famous Flying Dutchman in 1850 was three minutes. One hundred years later Galcador won the Derby of 1950 in two minutes thirty-six seconds, which suggests that in a modern classic the Flying Dutchman would be outclassed.

Intensive breeding for height and speed meant the gradual elimination of Arab influence, although the prepotency of the breed is such that many thoroughbreds still retain Arab characteristics. Inbreeding produced defects of bone and a gradual leaking of stamina; a policy which might seem suicidal but was encouraged by the number of races in Britain for big prizes over short distances. The sprinter became more profitable than the stayer. By the middle of the twentieth century it had become sadly apparent that the modern thoroughbred, although faster over short and middle distances than any in the history of horse breeding, had become prone to those very defects of bone, wind and temperament from which the genuine Arab remains free.

Many explanations are offered in the Sunday talk;

including the over-racing of horses which are officially
two years old but might be appreciably less because the
age of every thoroughbred officially dates from January
1st of the year in which it was foaled. This means that a
horse foaled in April is four months old at birth; that
when it first races as a two-year-old it might be twenty
months or less. Other acknowledged causes are a gradual
shift of emphasis, so that the profit motive has become
dominant. What began as a sport has become an indus-
try, with the further complication that racing is in-
separable from gambling, which in all walks of life and
at all times in history has been a corrupting influence.
There's deep dismay in the Sunday talk when men consider what has happened to the deep and powerful
dream of producing perfection and of watching it
grow.

Much of the Sunday talk is expressed in the special
language which horsemen have inherited, as actors have
inherited the language of the theatre and seamen the
language of the sea. It is a spoken language, seldom written and diminished by print; occasionally distinguished
by a phrase which has the glow of rough-and-ready
poetry. One such phrase is 'set a horse fair', which seems
to dignify part of daily routine.

A horse is set fair when it returns from exercise. Its
saddle patch and girth stains are sponged with warm
water; dried with wisps of hay or straw or perhaps
scraped with a curved scraper; brushed quickly to take
out shreds of straw and crumbs of dried sweat. Its
summer sheet or winter rug is replaced and the horse
made comfortable. Soiled straw has been already removed. Clean is forked around the walls and on top,

while the semi-stained remains beneath, next to the floor. A net is stuffed with fresh hay. The water trough or bucket is refilled; the head-collar is removed; the horse released to drink. Removal of the head-collar is symbolic. It informs the horse that work is over; that it is free to inspect the world from its half door, to rest with a back foot poised in the classic stance, perhaps to pull faces at the stable cat. A yard in which all the horses have been set fair is a quiet place.

'Racking up' is the phrase for tethering; either by chain or by nylon cord attached to a staple in the wall. The old-fashioned method was by rope, put through a hole and secured by a wooden block. Whatever the method, to rack short is to risk injury to spine or neck if the horse jumps backward. Many horses will respond belligerently to a short rope as a dog can be made bad tempered by a short chain. Some prefer to be racked in such a position that they can see the door and identify footsteps and satisfy their curiosities. Others prefer not to be racked at all, resisting any restriction but submitting to whatever you want as soon as they are free.

'Doing over' is a light grooming; 'strapping' is a much more strenuous form, part of the daily routine in stables where the owner insists on a healthy shine of the skin as well as of the coat. The difference between 'strapping' and 'grooming' is that while the purpose of one is to keep an animal clean, the purpose of the other is to stimulate the blood and to tone the muscles; rather like girls brushing their hair a hundred times or men submitting to massage after a Turkish bath. 'Strapping' is man's work. Few boys who are small enough to be potential jockeys have the necessary strength; a fact which American

stables recognize when they employ Negroes who are tall
enough to see the back of a big horse and strong enough
to maintain the essential rhythm despite the sidling and
fretting which rises at times in a crescendo. It's not unusual for a horse to kick six feet high and coconut mat-
ting is sometimes attached to walls or partitions to
prevent damage to legs and hooves.

'Off' is the righthand side; 'near' is the left, from
which you mount and on which all equipment is buck-
led. 'Turn away' describes the turning of a horse to
grass; sometimes for a holiday, sometimes to recuperate
after injury. The holiday is over when it is 'brought up
from grass'; often fat and mellow, unrecognizable as the
grimacing villain of the strapping sessions. 'Tack' is the
term for equipment. It is an abbreviation of 'tackle', as
in 'fishing tackle'. The tack room is the place where
martingales are hung and saddles are placed on wooden
or metal frames; where bridles are taken to pieces for
cleaning with sponge and saddle soap. Years ago bits
were cleaned with silver sand and by chains of small
mesh. The groom suspended the bridle from a hook in the
ceiling and half sat in the knotted reins; as proud of tack
for carriage horses as a butler of the family silver.

An unfit horse is said to be 'thick' in its wind; in need
of a steady canter to 'open the pipes'. My favourite
among the graphic phrases is 'swing on', exactly con-
veying the exhilarating action of a fit horse as it swings
into the 'daisy cut', which is a low, economical stride,
wasting no time in the air. If it 'puts its toe out' it is
making the most of that stride, but the 'star gazer' is for
ever looking upward, too nervous or excited or perhaps
too stupid to keep its eyes on its work.

One topic which has been argued for generations is the age of a horse in comparison with man. A persistent fallacy is that one year invariably equals seven. The fact is that the ratio varies with age and any comparison can only be generalization. The yearling is about as far advanced in its development as a child of seven; so that to ride a yearling or to inflict any weight on its back is as criminally stupid as it was, a hundred years ago, to compel seven-year-old boys to work in factories and fields. They suffered permanent injury less from having to work hard than from having to work at all.

At two years old the horse resembles the fourteen-year-old boy; capable of strenuous exercise but prone to injuries which might seem superficial yet become serious in later years. For this reason the horse which races at two years old is often 'old' in its legs when it is still immature. At three, the horse approximates a man of twenty; approaching the peak of its strength physically yet without that maturity which comes with experience and cannot be borrowed. At four, the fit horse, if it has been well cared for and has escaped injury to its back, legs or wind, resembles an athlete of about twenty-four; combining strength with experience yet still developing physically as well as mentally. A horse can grow an inch between its fourth and fifth year. Often it broadens to become more robust.

At five, the horse equals a man of twenty-six; at six, a man of thirty; at seven, a man of thirty-three. Strength and experience have fused into a confidence which makes it able to do with style what it only thought it could do two years before. Seven is often the year of achievement for steeplechaser, hunter, show jumper or polo pony. A year later it equals a man of thirty-five. It has reached its peak and is unlikely to improve. For about two years it might hold its own, but at eleven, the deterioration begins and can be rapid, so that within a season the twelve-year-old steeplechaser is trying to step on shadows which would have been far behind in its prime. At fourteen, the old campaigner approximates a man of fifty; ready for retirement in its body although still defiant in its spirit, capable even of brief bursts during which it seems to be 'as good as ever'.

At sixteen, there's no denying it; the horse is old, 'knocking sixty' in human terms, made slow by arthritis, its joints permanently swollen by the memory of old blows, its nostrils dribbling so that like many old men it begins the day with a cough. Extreme age shows first in a horse's wind and legs; whereas in mankind it shows in the heart and in a hardening of the arteries. Its teeth become a tobacco-stained yellow and are very worn. Its appetite might still be good but it has difficulty in masticating lightly crushed oats. The thoughtful owner dampens all its food and keeps it well rugged in winter. The old-age pensioner winces from fibrositis in knees and shoulders; the retired horse suffers from the equivalent and nothing which you do can protect it fully from the cruelties of age.

At twenty, the horse equals a man of seventy; stiff and often sore, yet still bright in its eye and ready to share a joke. But when you say that a horse at twenty-five is as near the end as a man of seventy-five, someone in the Sunday talk will remember horses still hunting at twenty-five; mares over thirty regularly giving birth to healthy foals. These exceptions are sufficiently numerous to expose the perils of dogmatic generalization. Much depends on the breed, the care, the feeding, on the freedom from abuse in its juvenile years.

It's when your horse is between twenty and twenty-five that you face the ultimate responsibility of ownership. You have had its good years. Now you become reluctantly aware that although its eyes are sharp, it is increasingly nervous of rain and wind, stiff in its back legs and afflicted by coughing, perhaps bleeding from a nostril after only mild exercise. You might even hear it groan when the blacksmith bends a foreleg to trim a foot. That groan is eloquent. The horse is a brave animal and does not readily complain. Any sound is a confession and the humane owner needs to heed it, then to wonder if it is necessarily true that any life is better than none.

Men cannot agree about this in the Sunday talk. Some advocate 'turning away' an old favourite, until it is found dead from 'natural causes'. Others believe that 'natural causes' can be slow and cruel. They consider it preferable to send the favourite to fair or market, since its carcass is still valuable. Dealers bid for old horses because the horse is the only animal whose meat improves with age.

My belief is that to condemn a horse to the grass of retirement is to condemn it also to rain and cold and humiliation; while to dispatch it to a market in the hope of receiving payment for the carcass is morally wrong since you can have no control over what happens between the hour of sale and the day of slaughter. When I had to have an old horse 'put down', I tried to ensure that it never heard a strange voice; that the shot was fired while its head was down to its favourite food. I asked an expert huntsman to fire the shot. The carcass was given to the hunt kennels in acknowledgement of his services and of his courtesy to the horse in the final minutes. I tried to do it 'right', to believe that it was merciful. But it still seemed a kind of murder. I imagine it is a day of grieving in many families when an old favourite has to be destroyed.

Between eleven and noon on a Sunday morning is the time for walking thoroughbreds to grass. There's a deep sense of leisure as you hold the leading tape and listen to a descendant of Hyperion cropping steadily, as serious about grass as any pony. It need not be good grass. Verge grass will do; or hedgerows which offer a cheap miscellany, although you need to keep a sharp eye for foxgloves, ragwort, rhododendron, laurel, laburnum, boxwood, aconite, even lupins. The most perilous poison is yew. A horse which eats it will be apparently unaffected for about half an hour, then might drop dead. It's not always realized that a horse has little discernment; that out of curiosity or perversity it will eat withered clippings while neglecting food more appetizing. The 'scarlet pimpernel' is another poisonous plant and farmers on the Pacific coast of North America call it the 'poison weed'.

We cut grass for horses which are sick or lame; cutting it with a scythe because a machine chews it and bruises it and horses are plainly disappointed by grass tipped from a mower. Lawn grass is dangerous because it might contain poisonous clippings. Tufts, dragged up with the earth still clogging the roots, supply the salt which in my childhood Pleasant found in the earth of her mangolds. Lame horses will beguile an hour or more poring over tufts and chewing the earth until mud shows in the corners of their mouths.

Sunday morning ends with the midday feed. During the afternoon heads are withdrawn from half doors. The horses are dozing. The yard dog is curled in straw in winter or sprawled on cold stone in summer. The stable cat lies pawless and eyeless on a ledge, too tired to be tantalized by plump fantails fluttering from the roofs. There is that silence which nature likes and which links today with Rome in A.D. 37; when to disturb the Emperor's horses from their afternoon dozing was an offence punishable by death.

13

THE MAKING OF A STEEPLECHASER

IT was the stride which decided me. I remembered an Irish voice saying if they can walk, they can gallop, and this horse could walk. She was a brown mare with a white star and a thin trickle of blaze, like a dribble of whitewash. She walked into the preliminary ring as though she owned it.

We were at Ascot for the June sales. Over a hundred horses were assembled for auction. They had come from breeders, from flat race stables and National Hunt stables. Possibly three times as many potential buyers were gathered on wooden benches around the auction ring or were leaning on paddock rails to watch and talk and to glad-hand friends whom they hadn't seen since the sale at Sandown.

A catalogue gave details of each horse; its pedigree, the achievements of its immediate ancestors, highly optimistic assessments of its potential. Some were declared to have such potential that you wondered why anyone could wish to sell. The explanations which the catalogue offered did not seem entirely adequate. 'Sold to dissolve a partnership' or 'Owner going overseas'. An Irish officer confessed to me that he had another reason; his wife's parents. Half the fun of a sale is reading the blarney or listening to it. The Irish are, of course, best at it.

We had ringed three possibles in the catalogue, with a large question mark against each because no vendor is going to confess troubles of wind or shoulder, splints in the forelegs, swollen hocks or sore spines; although reputable breeders announce the more obvious vices, including weaving and crib-biting. You have to find out the rest, exploring by hand and eye, as suspicious as those traders of forty years ago used to be when they bought vanners at the horse fair. The conditions have changed, but the scepticism is identical. You don't believe a word and the vendor knows it yet keeps talking, hoping less to convince than to distract you from discovering the lump behind the saddle or the sore ears which suggest ear-ache.

We had come disconsolately from the numbered boxes in which horses can be identified. None of our 'possibles' bore more than a passing resemblance to the eulogies. Others which were clean of limb and impeccably bred would be sought by buyers from overseas. Fast hurdlers and staying steeplechasers were in demand and prices promised to be high. We wanted a potential steeplechaser for about £300. Professional friends said we hadn't a chance, convincing us that we had made a long journey for nothing.

Then this dark-brown mare came striding into the preliminary ring, offering herself for inspection. I studied her from a distance in growing astonishment; like a film director who seeks someone to play a part and finds her in a nameless nobody. She was hidden in the catalogue. We had to fumble the pages to find the details; an unbroken four-year-old by an unfashionable stallion out of an unknown mare. Only her grand-dam had shown ability over fences. There was some history of minor success over four miles or more, but what could be said was disposed of in a few lines. She'd been in a field since her birth, the process of breaking having been interrupted by foot-and-mouth restrictions the previous winter.

The frugality of information was ominous. Moreover, her mane and tail were plaited; which can be a device to hide an affliction of the skin, perhaps dermatitis or sweet-itch. She was fat and clumsy, but high in the wither and strong of back. You could visualize the power behind the saddle. She went by with head high and ears alert, her eyes warm with interest. It must have been the first time she had heard so many sounds or seen so many faces; yet significantly she was not alarmed. You could see the courage.

My uncle in Pembroke, the one who made a small

fortune selling reels of cotton to the isolated, was speaking from the dead; pointing to the black legs and black feet, urging me to make sure. I ducked under the rail for close examination. Her forelegs were thin and hard, with prominent tendons. Her feet were cold. I heard my grandfather grumbling about inadequate bone, but the uncle in Pembroke was pleased. Other voices crowded my head, warning me that the making of a thoroughbred needs time, hundreds of hours; and who would help? My two sons were still at school; their experience necessarily limited to ponies and to 'made' steeplechasers. Voices stressed the demands on time and ingenuity and patience. They predicted failure.

But something had happened. While agreeing with them, admitting that it would take months, perhaps years, I was moving into the crowd around the auction ring. The bidding began at ninety, suggesting that few wanted the trouble of breaking and making. Only two signals came from the faces as the bidding crept up to a hundred and ninety guineas. Someone dropped out and I came in, matching the bids in jumps of ten until we reached two hundred and ninety. I hesitated and made what promised to be my final throw. My rival also hesitated, so long that I thought the mare was mine. But the unseen face bid again, pushing the price to three hundred and ten. My response was to increase the jump from ten to twenty, the price to three hundred and thirty.

It's an old tactic, but it worked. A bid of three hundred and thirty guineas betrayed my determination to my rival and my folly to my friends. Suddenly I was the owner of an unbroken four-year-old of sixteen-three

hands, with little to commend her except wide head and
bold eyes, high wither, black legs, cold feet and an ag-
gressively long stride. Some of my ancestors were ap-
proving, if for the wrong reasons. The old lady who had
sat in the dark and listened to the coach horses was glad
because I would 'give it a good home'. My grandmother
approved because even a young horse must be safer than
one of those terrible cars; while my mother seemed
pleased because there was beauty in the mare's stare,
reminiscent of Pleasant in the old days.

Only my friends kept shaking their heads. They had
hoped I would bring back an immediate winner, from
the success of which they might profit. They saw
nothing to be excited about in a ponderous substitute.
My sons wondered what their mother would say, for she
had already said plenty about riding thoroughbreds
through modern traffic. In the anticlimax which follows
the triumph of purchase. I came face to face with the
first of what promised to be many problems; getting her
home, since she had never travelled so far and might not
even enter the trailer.

She came to the ramp and stopped, needing time to
consider. We filled a hay-net and hung it where she
could see. We widened the adjustable partition, like
widening a door in welcome. My son walked up and
down, showing her that it was safe. She put a foot on it,
advanced a stride and waited, looking beyond us for the
horses with which she had come, for the faces which she
remembered. She neighed in bewilderment. It was an
imploring sound.

The transistor helped. She was interested by saxo-
phones playing a June-and-moon song from the 1930s.

She moved forward slowly and Mark held her while the partition was adjusted. The ramp was lifted. She tried to lurch backwards but Mark plucked hay from the net and tempted her; remaining with her during the journey of eight hours. We drove carefully, never more than thirty-five miles an hour, but she staggered and lurched, as precarious as a traveller in the corridor of a train. We reached home with relief.

Other horses and ponies were at their doors, made curious by the vehicle, made jealous by hoof-beats coming in. The mare gave them a cursory glance and walked into the new box. She looked at the fussed-up straw, the water bucket and hay-net, at the trough with damp bran waiting. She heaved a long sigh and widened her hind legs to pass urine. The absence of fuss was typical. Within minutes she was eating. An hour later we heard her dragging up the straw and preparing to lie down.

Her first need was a companion. In the morning we introduced her to a chestnut pony. They touched noses and exchanged breaths, stiff with doubt until abruptly they decided. The chestnut reached up to rest the side of his face against her neck and she looked above him, immediately defensive and protective. She followed the pony to the meadow and grazed for two hours, ready to be caught when he was caught. It seemed incredible that yesterday she had been at Ascot, looking for someone to assume ownership.

We gave her time to recognize footsteps as well as voices; to see her companion being saddled and ridden; slowly to understand that when the chestnut left the yard, it was not for ever. She waited for him intently, listening and calling, calling in a different way when she heard him; a piercing, urgent neigh, possessive and commanding.

Her education continued with frequent handling in the stable; reaching for her ears and scratching the tuft of mane on her poll. She liked this. She lowered her head and nudged for more, sometimes bending a foreleg so that her whole body leaned downward in a circus gesture. We rewarded her with apple.

Some owners are suspicious of any system of reward, but this is how circus horses were trained in the days of the travelling circus; how police horses are still trained to a high degree of obedience. It seemed reasonable to please her if she pleased us. In a matter of days she was giving up her feet for cleaning; screwing her eyes and wrinkling her nostrils in anticipation of the sponge; looking around in surprise when we lifted her tail to sponge her dock. The water was always warm. The reward was always punctual.

Caring for her required about three hours a day. She was given hay and damp bran as well as two hours of grass. She drank little, in the fashion of horses which graze regularly; but we kept the water bucket full because a horse's body is eighty per cent water and to be deprived during day or night makes a big horse bad-tempered. We introduced her to the bridle by introducing her to black treacle. She sucked it and slobbered over it and nudged for more. We smeared it on an eggbut snaffle and held the framework of the bridle in front of her, letting her smell the treacle and think about it, taking the bit when she took what she wanted.

The bit rings chimed as she slobbered. She was

interested by the merry sounds, continuing to chew the bit long after the smears of black treacle were gone, seeming to enjoy the chiming of the rings. Not until she took the bit without suspicion did we slip the framework over her ears. Her first reaction was indignation. She stared with swollen eyes, shaking her head and grimacing. But an animal can think of only one thing at once; as she chewed, the taste of treacle became more interesting than the pressure around her ears. When we slid the bridle down and let the bit fall out, there was dismay in her face because we were taking away what she wanted.

We were nervous about the padded roller. This is a webbing strap, with pads shaped to fit behind the wither. We showed it and she smelled it. We moved sideways to place it on her back and she stiffened, her strength coiled in a spring. We placed it on her back and eased down the strap on the other side. We reached for the strap and drew it up, fastening it to the first hole. It was still very loose but the slight pressure was frightening. She couldn't believe it. Her eyes bulged in incredulity. Suddenly she realized and her response was thunderous. Only a youth, quick on his feet and strong, could have moved with her as she whirled and stamped and cringed and kicked. Mark kept a hand on the headcollar during thirty seconds of crisis.

Gradually the storm eased. She began to get used to it, to admit that it wasn't so terrible or humiliating. We watched intelligence conquer the panic in her eyes. After a few minutes she was distracted by the stable cat which scrambled over the half door, indifferent to the turmoil, interested only by what crumbs of wealth might

be in the trough. It moved towards the trough with delicate precision, ignoring the stupid horse which was
making such a fuss. It found crumbs of bran and
crouched over them. The ticking of its tongue seemed to
be reproving.

The mare stared at the cat a long moment, then re-
sumed her protests. But the interruption had made a
difference. Her protests lacked conviction. She seemed
aware of the cat's disdain and lowered her head towards
it, seeking sympathy, begging it to look up, to see the
humiliating thing around her belly. The cat crouched
lower from the mare's breath but there was no sympathy
in its glance.

From that moment the mare gave in, confining her
protests to token demonstrations. She allowed us to
tighten the roller gradually until it was almost as tight as
girths would need to be.

Any weight on her back was new; even a summer
sheet, made of linen and fastened at the chest. She sank
to her knees and rolled, forcing it askew, seizing an end
with her teeth and trying to drag it off. The night-rug
was heavier and provoked a longer fight. No lesson was
easy, yet her reaction was never sullen or prolonged. We
were encouraged by her good nature, which forgave
each indignity as soon as her indignation was exhausted.

Soon she was accepting the saddle and a gradual
tightening of the girths. We walked her with the stirrups
removed and with a head-collar over the bridle; encouraging her to associate equipment with quiet ambles
through the lanes, during which her ears were turning
all ways, as sensitive as radar to sounds in front, on either

side and behind. In this slow and casual way she became accustomed to a weight on her back and pressures on her belly, to quiet movements of the flexible bar within her mouth. Always the chestnut walked in front, showing her how easy it was, disgusted by any display of temperament.

She was shod on her forefeet. The farrier came to the yard with a portable forge and she smelled the fire, listening to the iron chime of the tool box, the bronchial pant of the bellows. She was more interested than alarmed. We held her head, talking all the time, while the farrier asked for a foot and pared the horn. She looked down at his sweat-stained shirt and tried to pluck the string of his sheepskin apron; still without alarm as he brought a hot shoe and applied it. The fuss of smoke was sudden. She flinched and stared, on the edge of rebellion. You could see the fright trembling beneath her shine.

It was then, perhaps, that our voices made the difference. In a strange forge she might have fought, but the fact of a familiar environment, among voices which she knew and trusted, gave her confidence. She remained rigid while the shoes were nailed and the points rasped. You could hear the knocking of her heart.

Iron shoes gave her walk a new importance. She was startled by the clamour. Two weeks later shoes were added to her back feet, enabling her to be walked regularly on tarmac. She was learning a great deal, but one September afternoon the luck changed abruptly.

None saw what happened, so none can be sure. What is certain is that at half-past three she was dozing in her box, head low and dreams in her eyes. Five minutes later she was wet with sweat and shivering. The theory is that she was stung on the foreleg by a wasp and aimed kicks at the pain, striking with a back foot made formidable by new iron. Random kicking bruised the bone below the knee, causing a lump which hardened to a 'splint'. Many horses work freely despite permanent enlargements, but this lump was so near the back of the knee that we feared her galloping action would be impaired. There was despair in the family as we acknowledged that her career as a steeplechaser might be already over.

Our first need was to confine the lump. Rest was essential. We used a thin brush to paint on a veterinary preparation which she hated. She learned to recognize the bottle, reaching her foreleg in a long, sparring motion to box it away. We bought her co-operation with carrot, encouraging her to associate one with the other; as trainers of police horses persuade beginners to associate what they relish with the terrifying din of rattles and whistles.

For about six weeks she grazed a flat field by day and dragged hay from her net at night. She became bored and petulant as the leg improved. During the seventh week she was ready for slow work and by the end of November we were able to begin again. The lump was permanent but small. She seemed to have forgotten it. Two months later she was attending hunt meets for the experience of moving among other horses and ponies, rather than for serious hunting. She was excited by the hunting horn and by the clamour of hounds, yet was never beyond the control of a schoolboy.

Her manner changed as her meals were increased to

four a day and her ration of oats slowly increased to
eight pounds. She was also given a proprietary brand of
nuts, containing essential minerals; carrots, honey, cod
liver oil and malt; hay made of rye grasses and a little
clover. A salt lick was permanently in a corner of her
trough. She became more demanding and less sociable,
conscious of her increasing power and prone to demon-
strate it at the wrong times.

Schooling began with a pole about six inches high,
from which she graduated to hurdles varying in height
from eighteen inches to three feet. Her jumping was in-
stinctive. She leaned back on her hocks and hoisted herself up and over, without concern for economy yet with
massive generosity. Slowly she passed from hunter to
steeplechaser, although the progress was not as fluent as
it might appear.

We were hindered by frost and mud, since to jump a
horse over even small obstacles when frost is in the earth
is to risk damaging forefeet and pasterns; while to jump
in mud is to risk a slip in the instant of take-off or a long
slide in the act of touch-down. Many show jumpers
evade the vagaries of winter by being schooled under
cover on tracks of peat or sawdust. But the steeplechaser,
like the hunter, needs to be exposed to the conditions
which it will have to encounter during the racing season.
Changes of conditions encourage versatility. We found
that the mare moved freely only when the earth was soft,
that she galloped best on the tidal sands of West Country
beaches.

Twice a week she was taken to the sea, concluding
each session with a splash through the shallows when the
sea was calm or through pools orphaned by the receding

tide when the waves were high. Sea water, containing salt and iodine, proved good for her legs, slicking them to a black shine. In all this work she was accompanied by older horses or by her favourite pony, for one of the golden rules is that young horses must not be worked alone.

Her appearance changed so gradually that we were not fully aware of the difference until we compared photographs taken in September with others taken in March. She was not only slimmer of body, strong of neck and more muscled behind the saddle; she had become refined, so that her nostrils were sharply etched and her eyes bolder, her ears more acutely tuned to sounds. Simultaneously she had become moody, inclined to restlessness and impatience, especially when she was in season.

Fillies and mares come into season between late February and July at intervals of about three weeks. During these periods they are often sullen or depressed, sometimes excited to sudden squeals or to random kicking. One of the hazards of preparing a mare for racing is that she will prove less dependable than a gelding.

The mare was ready for racing by the end of April. She had learned to jump at speed, taking hurdles of three and a half feet in her stride. She had learned to face flapping flags; to gallop on left-handed and right-handed circuits; to respond to the slightest touch on her mouth; to match strides with older horses and to anticipate the bends, so that she did not lose yards by running wide. In all her serious work she was ridden by my son, Mark, who held a permit to ride as an amateur and had ridden other horses in about twenty races.

We decided to run her in a hurdle race for novices of four years old and upwards which had never won. It was only a humble race at a small West Country meeting, yet it would be the biggest test of her life so far. She knew that something special was about to happen, stamping around her straw in impatience, then darting to her half door and peering at the sky. Shoes were removed from her feet and racing plates of aluminium were substituted. She was excited by the sudden lightness. Her trembling was like the feel of music in a violin.

She heard the travelling box before we did. It came slowly down the hill and as the sounds crept nearer, she began to fret, her head wagging and ears back, her forefeet stamping like stepping on fire. Other horses looked out like neighbours from windows, wondering what the fuss was about and preparing to be jealous. We led out the chestnut pony. The mare began to neigh, sure there must have been some mistake, that she should be coming to. We held the pony at the ramp of the vehicle and led the mare towards it. She picked up her feet in a lilting melody, surprised by shoes as light as dancing pumps, flying her tail so that it poured in a black storm from the funnel of red bandage.

Damp straw had been scattered on the ramp. The pony climbed without hesitation and passed to one side of the padded partition. The mare stumbled in pursuit and passed to the other. It was all over in a minute. We were relieved, for some horses are bad loaders, so nervous of travelling that they fret themselves to a lather before they leave home.

We loaded the usual equipment: bridle and racing boots, paddock sheet, and anti-sweat sheet, rubber buckets, sponges, scraper, first-aid chest, a hay-net for the homeward journey. Five minutes later we were away, travelling slowly, acutely aware of the horse in the back and of what might happen when she realized her destination. She had never seen a racecourse. She might become half-crazy with excitement or stupid with fright or stubborn. The possibilities were running through our heads as we released the bolts and lowered the ramp.

Her astonishment was immediate. She tried to see and hear everything at once; the footsteps and shouting, the cars and flags and faces, the trot of other horses. But she didn't forget all she'd been taught. She didn't blunder around or become stupid. She placed her forefeet carefully on the ramp and leaned her weight and came down as nimbly as a dancer, swanking her tail as she turned, her head high and nostrils as wide as trumpets.

My son, Andrew, led her to the racecourse stables. A numbered box was reserved like a room in an hotel. I collected the key and signed the book, again like an hotel. Security guards, like private detectives, checked our credentials. She passed along the tarmac path between the boxes and ducked into the one which from that instant became hers. She smelled the wood shavings and turned around and stared, listening to horses beyond the partitions as she waited for the pony.

But we couldn't bring the pony to racecourse stables. The chestnut had to remain in the vehicle, nibbling hay and yawning. When the mare realized this, she dragged Andrew to the door and peered out, crying for the pony which had shared almost every experience since June. A microphone voice was a distraction. It was reading the runners for the first race and seemed to come from somewhere high, like the voice of Jehovah in the Old Testament. The mare looked for it, as fascinated as she had been by voices from a radio.

Horses went out looking glossed and came back wet and exhausted. Some were hurt. Several were bleeding. The mare watched them pass, her face showing what she was thinking. Occasionally she nudged Andrew, asking if he'd noticed. He remained with her all the time, for it's surely foolish to take a young horse to a strange place, then to walk away, if only for five minutes. The animal does not know that you will be back soon. Of course it feels abandoned.

She fidgeted throughout the final polishing, sidling and glaring and brandishing a back leg. We sponged her eyes and nostrils; lifted her tail and sponged her dock; picked up each foot and wiped it clean. We slipped the red reins over her head and put on the racing bridle. When she refused to part her teeth for the bit, I put a thumb at the back of her mouth and pressed down the lower jaw. The bit slipped over the tongue and she stood quietly while the throat lash was fastened. The leading rein was clipped to the off side bit ring and passed through to the near. Andrew took the tape while I threw on the paddock sheet, added the padded roller and slipped the cord beneath her tail.

By now she was fretting like a boxer within minutes of a fight. She blundered towards the paddock, excited by microphone voices. She looked what she was: a clumsy beginner, five years old yet much less experienced than many of that age, committed to her first test among twenty-six others, almost all of them older and much wiser.

Mark had weighed out on the official scales and was waiting with the racing saddle, weight cloth and number cloth. I collected them and beckoned Andrew to bring her to the saddling stall. She backed into it reluctantly, always nervous of what she could not see. Her number was twenty-three. She would carry eleven stone, but Mark's weight was little more than nine. The difference had to be made up partly by a saddle of about seven pounds, partly by thin circles of lead placed in the pouches of the weight cloth. There were two girths and, as a further precaution, a surcingle which passed over the saddle.

She fretted and kicked, enjoying the thunder of her hooves in the wooden partitions. Her ears did not come forward until she recognized Mark coming from the jockeys' room. It was Mark who had first got a leg over her; who had ridden her among traffic and to hounds; who had persuaded her to jump the first nursery pole. Their association had been long and amiable. She thought of him in terms of sport and hunting horns and salt beaches, of walking out to grass on Sunday mornings. She stared at him intently, surprised by the racing colours and satin cap. Few in the crowd could have known they were an unusual partnership; the least experienced horse and the youngest rider.

She returned to her place in the parade, alternating moments of exuberance with long periods of reflection during which she studied the scene, photographing it with her memory. From the first she had proved vain as well as intelligent, most petulant when she supposed she was being ignored. She plainly welcomed so many faces like an actress welcoming an audience. What pleased us most was the sharp intelligence of her ears, because it's important for a horse to have brains as well as ability and courage. In steeplechasing there is a great deal to learn and even a hurdle race over two miles and eight flights of hurdles would tax her concentration. She would need to be bold, distracted neither by others falling nor by jealous bumping for that narrow strip on the inside of each bend. She would need to do what she had been taught and perhaps a little more, all of it at a speed of thirty-five miles an hour. There would be no time for hesitation. If she chickened out at the first hurdle she could be brought down by other horses and might kill the boy.

All this was at the back of my mind as I slid off the paddock sheet and tightened the surcingle and boosted Mark to the saddle. She felt the tension and wanted to be away. Her instinct was to be first out of the paddock. Reluctantly she accepted her humble place in the long line and passed in front of the stands. The leaders turned and cantered towards the start. She followed, her ears pricked and eyes serious, her head low in the fashion of a potential steeplechaser.

Mark took her to the first hurdle, letting her examine it and consider what it meant. She showed her contempt by trying to snatch a shred of gorse. They came back to the gate, where the starter called the roll. Jockeys answered, 'Here, sir,' like obedient boys at school. Horses faced the long tape. At the touch of a lever it rattled upward and the mare was taken by surprise. For the first time she showed fright. Her back cringed. She hesitated, unwilling to pass beneath the thing which for a throbbing second had seemed alive. Other horses plunged forward and she followed. She was last as they approached the first hurdle.

I wanted to close my eyes, because anything might happen. If we hadn't taught her well enough, she might falter or stumble. If she wasn't brave enough or generous enough, she might swerve. But you can't close your eyes. You've got to watch.

I need not have worried. The mare didn't check or swerve or fumble. She took off in a flying leap, her neck long and head stretched, her lithe body giving every ounce. It was the most important jump of her life, confirming what we had thought from the first; that whatever qualities she might lack, she was a natural jumper, fired by the essential courage.

Within a few strides she was tracking the leaders, holding her own in the inevitable hurly burly. Through powerful glasses I saw her ears flatten in resentment of so many wanting her place. The truculence was typical. She jumped the second and third as well as she had jumped the first, then began to slow. We let out a howl of horror, supposing she was hurt. But the mare wasn't hurt, only more intelligent that we had thought.

At home her schooling stint had been over three hurdles. She guessed it must be the same here. Mark had to convince her there were more and when she saw the fourth, her response was immediate. She lengthened her stride and attacked it, putting in a leap which exposed her inexperience. It was much too high, taking out more than the obstacle was worth.

She remained on the heels of the leaders for a mile and a half. At the sixth hurdle the pace quickened. She couldn't adjust her stride as more experienced horses

began to pass on either side. She looked indignant and baffled, striving to give a little more but shackled by deepening tiredness. Mark let her finish easily and the welcome could not have been warmer if she had won.

She trotted back to the paddock, waited for the saddle to be removed, then trotted to the racecourse stables, too vain to admit tiredness. Her nostrils were as red as the inside of anemones, her veins were swollen and sides steaming. We found no cuts, no bruises. She wanted a drink. She also wanted her bridle to be removed and her face sponged, the trickles of sweat to be wiped from her back legs. Typically she wanted everything at once.

We sponged her with warm water, squeezing it between her ears so that streams ran down. She tilted her face and narrowed her eyes, her tongue trying to drink the dribbles on either side. We scraped her dry and put on the anti-sweat sheet and let her have a small drink. She passed out to the exercise yard and walked around, her tension uncoiling as slowly as a spring. Soon her body was dry, her eyes were quiet. She was giving in to her tiredness, asking to be taken home.

We took her home in the twilight and gave her warm mash, plenty of hay and water, a deep bed of straw. In

the morning she walked to the paddock for grass; ordinary food for a pony but a luxury to a racehorse after months of artificial foods. She looked different in the sunshine; more mature and sedate, glad to be home and resting like a soldier returned from battle.

Our friends asked what next and when? They were amazed when the answers were several months away; on the other side of summer, when autumn was in the trees and the hiss of rain was in the earth. Rain was essential because the next stage in her development was a race of two miles over twelve fences and the hard earth of summer might jar her forelegs. Time was equally important. She would need to be schooled over brushwood fences, including one with an open ditch and at least four feet high. There would also be a water jump, with a three-foot fence, the span about twelve feet and the water simulated by a polythene sheet pegged to the ground and giving a dull shine. It is a tactic used by duck shooters to decoy wild duck.

Part of the summer was spent in building strong, thick fences: more formidable than schooling hurdles yet not so formidable that she would be discouraged. Three were built in line over a straight stretch of five hundred yards; a hedge on one side to ensure that she did not swerve to the right, a big wing to ensure that she did not swerve to the left. We tried to make it as easy as possible, yet as she approached a steeplechase fence for the first time, you could see the anxiety in her face, the moment of cowardice when she did not think she could do it. In that moment she wanted to duck out or stop. She was forced onward, partly by the encouragement of horses which accompanied her on either side, partly by the determination of her rider. She gripped her courage and jumped. Suddenly she was on the other side. You could sense her relief: hear the excitement in her breathing like the pants of a breast-stroke swimmer who has survived the first few strokes.

It is a mistake to school horses too often or even to exercise them too often in the same field. They become bored by repetition. Yet it is important to strengthen a horse's jumping muscles; in the old phrase to get 'their jumping muscles up'. How can you do it without jumping? Work on steep hills is one way; perpetual climbing in which all the work is done by the strength behind the saddle. We kept her at it until you could see the muscles moving like a fish in a shallow river. Often she wanted to plunge up, to get it over; but the pace needed to be a steady walk, making demands of the right muscles while putting minimum strain on her legs.

Nothing was new to her now. She knew the fences and the degree of effort which each demanded. She knew how to canter seriously, with head low and eyes down, without need for martingale or any other restriction. Once a week she was galloped across tidal sand, her stride exultant yet economical, her face expressing indignation when other horses came alongside. Her drumming was a young sound in the ageless sand.

We entered her in several steeplechases for novices over two miles, waiting for what promised to be a comparatively easy race in a small field and on soft going. You have to be patient with a young horse. My sons were pressing me to take risks, but at the back of my mind were the voices of old men, counselling caution, recalling good horses which had been damaged by impatience. On the other hand it becomes increasingly easy to find excuses for doing nothing, striving to protect your horse as over-zealous parents try to shield their children from the pains of experience. I erred in this direction while my sons erred in another.

Finally she was declared to run in a novice steeplechase of two miles. The going was reported good to soft, which meant that she would leave imprints. In her final schooling session she jumped joyfully, seeming to be lit by a power which threatened to explode.

The substitution of plates for shoes informed her of what was about to happen. She waited at her half door; remembering the hired vehicle and listening for it, resisting travelling bandages on her legs and tail, vitally different from the horse of a year ago, so that she seemed not to recognize us nor to remember the hours we had spent scratching her poll in evening stillness. Our amiable mare had become a tyrant. It's what happens. You gain a racehorse and lose a pet.

She followed other horses to the ramp and passed to her side of the partition. She knew where she was going. Beneath the travelling rug the sweat began to trickle, leaving long, pale stains on her legs. Andrew stood at her head, his face near the knocking of her heart. A transistor played mild music. She tried to touch the box with her nose, perhaps amazèd that so many sounds could come from a thing so small. Quietly we raised the ramp, hoping that the transistor would distract her. Now my sons were relieved that we had chosen a meeting near home, that the journey would be of less than an hour; although an hour can seem long if your horse is trembling, if the travelling box is smelling of steam which shimmers like a mirage in the desert.

Andrew tapped the back of the cab, using the family code to inform us that she was distracted, as years ago the Exmoor had been. Only during the chatter of disc jockeys did she shift her weight from one leg to another. When the chatter went on too long she kicked the partition and the Irish grey answered. We heard the thuds and waited for Andrew to signal that all was well.

It was during this journey that I remembered the boy who had stood beside Loppy and had wondered about this sport which demands so much of horses. At ten years old I had been unable to understand my fascination. More than thirty years later I was equally bewildered; unable to reconcile pride in the careful preparation of a horse and deep delight in its well-being with a growing reluctance to take it to the races. The logical climax of months of preparation was this steeplechase. I should have been excited by the prospect of seeing the mare prove herself and simultaneously justifying the work and expense. Instead there was only anxiety, lit by images of disaster which pretended to be premonitions.

Long before we reached the racecourse I had begun to

understand why so many owners remain remote from their horses, placing them with licensed trainers and seeing them only at weekends or on race days. They do not become involved. Their affection is detached and this detachment is pleasant, enabling them to enjoy ownership, to discuss their horses light-heartedly, even to cope with mild teasing in the event of failure. It was different for me. I watched my horse and son go out of the paddock with the emotional confusion of a playwright who watches the curtain rise on his play.

There is pride among the playwright's alarms, for he knows that the work he has put into his play is good or at least as good as he can do; that the quality is being acknowledged and that the murmuring sounds are commendation. But at the back of his mask is the horror that with the rising of the curtain, his property, his creation – more than that, a part of himself – has passed beyond his control. There is nothing he can do; except watch and hope for a merciful conclusion.

I've watched the beginning of plays with no more apprehension than I watched the mare turn at the end of the parade and canter towards the start. Mark took her beneath the gate to the first fence. She repeated her gesture of contempt; trying to snatch a shred of brushwood. They came back for the roll call; to the quiet walk-around as the starter's assistant tightened surcingles and jockeys fidgeted their stirrup leathers. There was a minute of waiting while the starter climbed to his wooden platform. Near us officials were lowering number boards in preparation for the next race while bookmakers shouted and anxious faces looked up, their hands still raised like sinners begging salvation. I

wondered how many of the betting faces realized the
work which goes into the preparation of a horse; how
many cared about the risks which professionals and
amateurs were taking.

Always in the minute before the start I hate the sport
and despise the parasites who thrive on it. My wife
clutches my arm with fingers which tighten. Our colours
move to the inside, showing that our son has no intention
of conceding yards to professionals. The mare is on her
toes, expressing a tension which passes along the line.
We cannot see their faces, but we know that the boy is
grim and watchful, that the mare is big-eyed, ready to
trigger the power which we have slowly created. The
tape lurches up and they are away; eleven horses pounding to the first, eleven caps in a muddle, eleven hearts
hammering faster because one slip can mean disaster.

The risks are enormous and never the same as they
were yesterday or will be tomorrow. The brushwood
seems impossibly high as the mare reaches it. We close
our eyes, waiting for the racecourse commentator to
inform us; begging him to say it, to say it quickly, to say
it before our minds burst.

From a loudspeaker the racecourse commentator
says: 'All over the first'.

AFTERWORD

by MARK SMITH

The king was the first to notice the absence, although not quite understanding what it was that he had noticed. Very uncharacteristically, he left his trough after only a quick mouthful of oats and came to his half door with a slightly puzzled expression on his face. Peering out into the darkness he stopped chewing; ears and eyes straining to detect what it was that was amiss.

The impatient neighs of the Exmoor for her feed reminded him of the oats in his trough. But again after snatching another quick mouthful he stopped and stood quite still, head high, eyes staring and ears pricked. A distinctly worried look upon his face, he returned to the half door and stared a long stare towards the lighted back door of the house, as if waiting for someone to come out. After several seconds he screamed a long neigh into the still, dark, early morning – too piercing and distressed to be anything but the call of the desperate.

The yard fell silent. The chewing sounds that normally accompany feed-time stopped abruptly. The other horses stood, their mouths still half full of oats, their ears pricked, waiting for the king to repeat or elaborate on his call.

When he failed to do so they came, one by one, to their doors, anxious to know what was wrong. In a matter of seconds there was a head at every door – all straining to see or hear what it was that had so obviously upset the king. All were acutely aware that there was something wrong yet none but the king realized what it was – what was missing from the yard.

Finally the king turned from his door. The spell was broken. Then, like mourners after a funeral, the others drifted away, back to their troughs. The old king, however, was like the bereaved, still distressed when the funeral is over. He fretted in circles around his box, picking a quick bite from his hay net but then letting it hang from his mouth like the caricature yokel, as if thinking about what had been and what could never be again.

The work of the yard had to go on as usual that day because that was doubtless how Father would have wanted it. During the routine of stable work not only the king but all of the others as well, paid frequent visits to their doors to stare at the back door of the house, unable to believe his non-appearance.

Little things in the yard were different and they all reacted in their individual ways to these changes. The strong young mare aimed a kick at me with her forefoot when I omitted to give her a piece of carrot after I had finished picking out her feet, telling me that Father never forgot. The timid Irish grey flinched away when I was brushing near his ears, complaining that Father had always used a softer brush around these tender places. The Exmoor kicked at her door in a torrent of rage because she had never been left till last at feed-time before. They all missed the little extra fuss and attention which earned Father the descriptions of 'fanatical' and 'eccentric' from those who failed to understand his true love of horses.

The tragic death of their master unfortunately signalled the end of a glorious and bountiful era for the horses he owned. The financial commitments of so many horses were crippling without someone constantly writing about them and thus deriving indirect income from them as my father had. When it became clear that they would all have to go, I took six months' leave from my editorial career to supervise their sale, so that they would all go to the very best homes. It took several months but now this has been achieved, often at considerable financial sacrifice, for the best homes cannot always afford the best prices.

When I look back at the horses that he owned I immediately remember the first, which of course, he always considered to have been the best. She was an old mare, years past her best, but still with a zest for work. She and Father grew very attached as she taught his sons and daughters to ride properly. One summer night, when her work for the day was done, the mare was turned out in the orchard. Father always turned the horses out at night in the summer when there were no flies to plague them. Unlike most people, Father would curse the weather not when the gusts of sheeted rain swept up the valley, but when the sun beat down remorselessly, baking the ground too hard to risk galloping as well as bringing out the big, fat, parasite horse-flies.

This mare suffered from a heart attack that night and was lying prostrate where she had fallen, when my Father appeared in the morning. He hurried to her side, fearing that she was already dead. She raised her head and gave him a soft, half-choked nucker. Then her head fell back and it was over. Father considered it a great tribute that the mare had hung on grimly to that precious spark of life until she had his company to die in.

Now, as I wander around the deserted yard, remembering, I get nostalgic. I look over the door of the box where the little Dartmoor was kept. It had been a pigs' box, empty for years, when one day at a local sale, for no logical reason, I bought Juliet. She needed a box because it was winter and even Dartmoor ponies like to come inside when there is snow on the ground. So, in one afternoon of toil and endeavour, we converted that pig box into a box any pony could have been proud of. But we were in for a shock which made all of our efforts seem rather futile. The little pony, who we had thought would come racing to the gate of the orchard where we had turned her out, not only failed to do this but stubbornly refused to be caught at all. If you chased, she became frightened and ran. If you coaxed, she was suspicious and turned away. After all, she had a good orchard of grass, more than she'd had in a long time, and if she allowed herself to be caught she might not be given such freedom and wealth of grazing again. That night as the first flakes of a snowstorm floated innocently down into the yard a frightened little pony stood out in the orchard and shivered while the empty, freshly white-washed loose box stood waiting in the yard. Later she was to become the family pet described in this book, though she will never again share tea with us. It's pleasant to think she is not far away, at a riding school where she is giving five- and six-year-olds their first experience of riding.

I slide back the bolt of the box where the young hurdler once stood. The noise of the bolt shooting back echoes around the empty box with a hollow sound. When I think of the many times I came into this box to dress that little mare over, I remember how she used to squeal and squirm when you brushed under her belly, for she was very ticklish. The son of a Somerset vicar now owns her and is racing her over hurdles in Germany.

In the empty box where the strong young chaser stood, the chips out of the wall remind me how she used to kick out when you tightened the girths. Seeing the hook on the wall, I recall how adept she used to be at undoing the rope by which she was tied up. Often when you were grooming her you would suddenly realize that she was loose and could have kicked you at any time during the last couple of minutes. She is now in another racing yard running for her new owner.

The old king's box brings back most memories: that stiff bolt with the stop gone so that you invariably pulled it too hard and it shot right across the yard when it did finally come undone. There is the trough that the king used practically to jump into in his undying enthusiasm for food. It was in this box with the king that I learnt every trick in the book, every trick that it is possible to pick up in ten years in a racing stable. He was as clever on the racecourse as he was off it – never giving an ounce more than he had to but doing just enough to keep himself safe. In over seventy races he never fell, and he made my first few rides, the most important for anyone, real confidence-boosters. The king is now hunting in

Hampshire. His box is empty and weeds are starting to push their way around the doorposts.

Dartmoor was my Father's other great love. He knew and understood both the people and the terrain so well, having lived on or around it since his earliest days when he came to stay with his grandparents who farmed on the moor and, of course, owned Pleasant. From 1950 to 1960 he worked for local newspapers and, by the time he gave up journalism to concentrate on writing novels, he was undoubtedly an authority on Dartmoor and its people. His favourite period of history was the nineteenth century; this coincided with his observation that 'when you go up on to the moor it is like going back a hundred years'. Although the settlements on the moor have become infinitely more civilized in the last ten to fifteen years, there are still many hamlets without mains, water or electricity. The open moorland, of course, has changed very little in the last thousand years, and it was here that he could really get away from it all to sort out the problems of his latest book. One of his favourite spots was on the steep slopes of the Dart valley above Dartmeet, where he would sit on the old coffin stone which lies there. The open moorland seemed to inspire him, and it must have been up here, while plotting his next book and thinking of his horses, that he was most contented.

COME DOWN THE MOUNTAIN BY VIAN SMITH · 25p
552 52033 0 · Carousel Fiction

The house had been empty for months, ever since the old man had died. The big bay horse had been left in the field, forgotten and neglected. Nobody owned him or acknowledged responsibility for him.

But Brenda looked for the horse each morning on her way to school and each evening on her way home. She worried about what would happen to him when winter darkened the moor. When she saw the horse lying on its side, his neck stretched, his head flat in an attitude of despair, Brenda knew she would have to defy her parents and the village – she *had* to save him.

HERACLES THE STRONG BY IAN SERRAILLIER · 25p
552 52034 9 · Carousel Fiction

Heracles was the son of Zeus, the Father of the gods, but he was born into a mortal family. The goddess Hera hated Heracles because he was not her own, and in a fit of spite and jealousy drove him blindly mad. Like a whirlwind Heracles raged through the palace and committed the most dreadful crimes.

Condemned by the gods, Heracles had no alternative but to accept his punishment and tackle the twelve seemingly impossible tasks set before him by the cowardly King Eurystheus.

THE ARABIAN NIGHTS: ALI BABA AND OTHER STORIES FROM THE THOUSAND AND ONE NIGHTS
THE ARABIAN NIGHTS: ALADDIN AND OTHER STORIES FROM THE THOUSAND AND ONE NIGHTS
BY AMABEL WILLIAMS-ELLIS · 30p
2 Volumes · 552 52036 5 · 552 52037 3 · Carousel Fiction

Long ago, there lived a powerful King. His beautiful Queen seemed to love him as dearly as he loved her; but one day he discovered that she had been conspiring with his enemies to poison him. Half-mad with rage, this King killed his treacherous Queen and vowed that each time he married, his new wife would be beheaded on the morning after the marriage. For some time the King kept his wicked vow. One day he ordered his Grand Vizier to bring him his eldest daughter, Shahrazad, to be his next Queen. Now Shahrazad was not only beautiful she also knew more than a thousand stories. She devised a plan using these stories to prolong her life and to stop the King fulfilling his vow. These two volumes include some of these tales.

**THE HOW AND WHY WONDER BOOK OF
WILD ANIMALS**   30p

552 86508 7

Information about many of the world's most interesting wild
animals, what they look like, where they live, how they hunt, what
they eat, their intelligence and means of protection – these are
some of the features that make this book both educational and
entertaining.

MALCOLM SAVILLE'S SEASIDE BOOK   30p
BY MALCOLM SAVILLE

552 54054 4   Carousel Non-Fiction

This book is a fascinating account of the sea and the seaside in all
its aspects and with Malcolm Saville as a guide, the seaside will
assume a new fresh face.